Suzy Gershman

BORN TO SHOP

NEW ENGLAND

The Ultimate Guide for
Travelers Who Love to Shop

3rd Edition

MACMILLAN • USA

*For Michael Gershman, whose second-favorite job
in the world is driving me around the back roads
of New England—with love and thanks for a
million wonderful miles. I love you forever. Moux.*

MACMILLAN TRAVEL
A Simon & Schuster Macmillan Company
1633 Broadway
New York, NY 10019

Find us on-line at **http://www.mgr.com/travel** or on America
Online at Keyword: **SuperLibrary.**

ISBN   0-02-860714-7
ISSN   1066-2782

Editor: Kelly Regan
Production Editor: Lynn Northrup
Copy Editor: Marianne Steiger
Design by George J. McKeon
Digital Cartography by Ortelius Design

SPECIAL SALES
Bulk purchases (10+ copies) of Frommer's travel guides are
available to corporations, organizations, mail-order catalogs,
institutions, and charities at special discounts, and can be
customized to suit individual needs. For more information
write to Special Sales, Macmillan General Reference, 1633
Broadway, New York, NY 10019.

Manufactured in the United States of America

CONTENTS

MAP LIST

WHAT THE SYMBOL MEANS

· ·

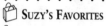 SUZY'S FAVORITES

Stores, restaurants, and accommodations you should not miss.

TO START WITH

The book you are holding is a special one to me because it is one of the last in the whole group of 10 books that make up the Frommer's *Born to Shop* series and as I finish this, it means that it's time to start painting the Golden Gate Bridge all over again and go back to revisions.

If you aren't used to the changes we've made with the Frommer editions, you'll notice a new format and a new front-of-the-book chapter with some "Best of" bragging to guide you toward my favorites in New England. I have a feeling that locals spend most of their winter fighting over who has the best, so these are just a few homegrown opinions from someone who really does live in New England.

This book has lots of space devoted to Boston (tons of changes there!) and much information about factory outlets, as New England is the most densely packed with outlets—and new ones keep popping up. There's also background on crafts, antiques, and your favorite Yankee villages, historic or not.

This book wouldn't have been possible without the help and devotion of my husband Mike, who drove me to many of these places, and our son Aaron, who hopes to go to college in Boston and has suddenly become more interested in that part of town. Thanks also to the gang at Filene's Basement for keeping me on top of things, and especially Pat Boudrot, who gets me invited to things like the opening of The Vault. Hugs to all my pals in Boston: Alix Gordon, Caron LeBrun, etc.

The cover was shot, as always, by Ian Cook, who came to Westport to catch me at my local pumpkin patch, Geiger's, just down the street from where I live.

Chapter One

· · · · · · ·

THE BEST OF NEW ENGLAND IN A NUTSHELL

·

New England encompasses a lot of territory; it is virtually impossible to pick the best of anything on a state-by-state basis. *Boston* magazine devotes an entire issue each year to merely "The Best of Boston," with hundreds of listings, so this section is merely a quick look at those places you should be certain to check out if you're in the area.

All stores and events mentioned below are described in more detail in their appropriate chapters; this is just to whet your appetite, help you plan your route, and get you going.

THE BEST SHOPPING EVENT
· ·

FILENE'S BRIDAL SALES
Boston, MA

BRIMFIELD ANTIQUES MARKETS
Brimfield, MA

I had to go with two listings here since they each highlight what I consider an important part of New England's legacy to shoppers everywhere. New England is big on special events—maybe since they invented Thanksgiving and it went so well they decided to keep on going.

The Filene's Bridal Sale is only for those in need (a small portion of those of you reading this book), but as theater, entertainment, and mayhem it is unparalleled in American retail history. I suggest you fly in for the sale if you are planning a wedding, stay at a hotel like Swissôtel Boston, which is a block from Filene's Basement and which provides special shopper's rates and discount coupons, and then stand in line and tough it out.

Brimfield is a series of markets and while it stretches for about 10 days, most of the markets last only 3 days each. It's a different type of madness, and actually is quite civilized except on opening day, when the barricades are broken down around 6am.

Both big-tent events are held a few times a year—the Bridal Sale four times a year and Brimfield three times a year (in May, July, and September).

THE BEST CUTIE-PIE STORE (CLOTHING)
. . . .

BRAMHALL & DUNN
Nantucket and Martha's Vineyard, MA

Sure, you know the key to being accepted in the "in" crowd at certain resorts is looking like you're a member of the clan, but did you know you can put it all together simply by shopping one handy store? Even if you buy nothing at Bramhall & Dunn, stop by to stare, touch, and admire the whimsy and sophistication.

THE BEST CUTIE-PIE STORE (HOME STYLE)
. . . .

LILLIAN AUGUST
Westport, CT

Lillian is a designer of fabrics and fine things. Her store puts it all together in a colonial French/country Americana/rich English sort of jumble that makes you yearn to empty your house and fill in with her goodies. Ask about the annual warehouse sale. Also note that next door to Lillian a very fine copycat store has sprung into being—**Henry Lehr Home.**

THE BEST CUTIE-PIE STORE (CRAFTS DIVISION)

CLAIRE MURRAY
Nantucket, MA

OK, so maybe you have to like hooked rugs in the first place and be a fool for American folk arts. I am; I do; I'm yours, Claire. Do-it-yourself kits as well as finished carpets are sold, along with other decorative touches. While there are a few Claire Murray shops dotted around New England, and even a real factory in New Hampshire, this particular store, in a lovely little house, gives new meaning to the word cute.

THE BEST FABULOUS FUNKY STYLE

NANTUCKET LOOMS
Nantucket, MA

This store is less cutie-pie and more about texture and touch and crafts and weaving and chenille and mohair and pieces of heaven.

THE BEST FASHION

LOUIS OF BOSTON
Boston, MA

From the mansion in which the store is located to its award-winning restaurant and the cutting-edge clothes for men and women, this is simply one of the best stores in all of America, let alone New England. Don't miss it for the world.

THE BEST RETAIL CONCEPT & SERVICE

L. L. BEAN
Freeport, ME

You have to give these guys credit for a move toward understanding shoppers and their needs. The store is open all the time; they have assorted niche catalogs for your every need; they are out to provide more service than you can imagine; and they even have a discount store a block away. L. L. Bean isn't about fashion, or even style; it's about a way of doing business and a way of simply being.

THE BEST FIND

APRIL CORNELL
Boston, MA

April Cornell is not new to business and you may have found her on your own; she has operated a small chain of stores called Handblock for many years. Most Handblock stores have been renamed for the designer, so don't get confused. The goods remain the same and are very special in terms of their color and vibrancy. This is the kind of store I'd like to find for you and send you to in every city I visit; it just feels special. Of the many April Cornell stores dotted around New England, the one in Faneuil Hall in Boston often serves as an outlet and unloads goodies at low prices.

THE BEST ANTIQUES TOWN (JUNKY & FUNKY)

ESSEX, MA

This town is about an hour north of Boston and well worth the drive—you may want to rent a U-Haul truck. The entire town is one store after another, but it's very low-key. You have to enjoy the search, the dust, and the deal.

THE BEST ANTIQUES TOWN (HIGH-END)

. . . .

WOODBURY, CT

Another town filled with dealers, but these are the fancy dealers with the good stuff and the high prices. No dust. Some deals.

THE BEST FACTORY-OUTLET MALL

. . . .

CLINTON CROSSING & WESTBROOK
Clinton, CT & Westbrook, CT

I don't mean this as a cop-out, but I find it takes a combination of these two to provide the one whole that truly satisfies me. These outlets are two exits apart off of I-95 (Exits 63 and 65). Taken together, they're all cute architecture (designed like Victorian train stations and villages), and high-end stores (J. Crew, Polo, Episode, Mal Cashmere, etc.), and they can be handled without too much difficulty since each outlet mall has only about 60 stores.

THE BEST FACTORY-OUTLET CITY

. . . .

MANCHESTER, VT

Let's face it: If you want a weekend devoted to New England charm, great shopping, and good eats, look no further than Manchester, the Equinox Hotel, and the scads of factory outlets dotted between Manchester Village and Manchester Centre.

THE BEST REAL-FACTORY SALE

. . . .

C. R. GIBSON
Norwalk, CT

This is the real thing—you have to get on the mailing list in order to know when the biannual sales are held. Gibson makes paper goods and sells them in bulk at rock-bottom prices from the warehouse. Highest possible quality in paper plates, napkins, wrapping paper, greeting cards, and Christmas everything.

THE BEST OFF-PRICE STORE

· ·

FILENE'S BASEMENT DOWNTOWN CROSSING
Boston, MA

The mother ship is very different from all the branch stores. While I don't pooh-pooh the branches, there is *nothing* like this store and their newest addition, The Vault, where very big-time designer merchandise is sold at low to embarrassingly low (for the designers) prices. Yes, I'm talking Ferragamo.

Chapter Two

. . . .

NEW ENGLAND DETAILS

WELCOME TO NEW ENGLAND

. . . .

New England: The very name is just foreign enough to arouse excitement . . . and yet nothing is more American. New England has been the American dream for more than 350 years.

Yes, they really do have covered bridges in New England. And whales. And blueberries. And cranberries . . . and a whole lot more. While your first thoughts may be of Pilgrims, changing seasons, and Paul Revere's ride, we're here to whisper a few other endearments in your ear:

- New England has more factory outlets than any other region of the United States—with more new outlets still opening.
- New England remains the core of colonial America; the antiques of yesterday and tomorrow are in ready abundance.
- New England is one of the leading crafts capitals of the world.
- New England is a mere 6 hours from Olde England and a world away pricewise—foreign visitors can expect the cost of goods to be dramatically cheaper.
- More and more cruise ships are coming to port in New England. Once limited to seasonal "Leaf Changing" cruises during late September and

early October, the area is suddenly a hot spot at most any time of the year. Now, major cruise companies—not those ferry companies—are bringing visitors to several ports every day.

So welcome to New England, a part of America that is distinctly different from the rest of America. Welcome to New England, which really does have things about it that are just like Olde England (just wait until you drive around your first rotary). Welcome to New England, where price and value merge. Welcome to my neck of the woods, the part of America where I live; to my town and my backyard. I can't wait to show you the neighborhood.

THE SHOPPING SCENE

Combine Yankee thrift with crafts villages, historical landmarks (all with gift shops), old brick warehouses, cutie-pie towns, Boston, and a zillion factory outlets, and you have a shopping scene unique to America and unique to the world.

There is an old Yankee saying: "Use it up, wear it out. Make it do or do without." And more people are now embracing that same philosphy at factory outlets and crafts fairs; they buy things that will indeed last and give pleasure along the way. No one has chicly threadbare cuffs anymore, now that there's a factory-outlet mall in every state.

Shopping in New England, of course, could be a full-time adventure. There's a vast amount of territory to see (and shop) in the six states that comprise New England—and then there are parts of upstate New York and provinces of Canada that are perfect complements. You could spend a lifetime exploring and enjoying the scenery . . . and the stores.

Even in my own village in Connecticut during the last year, tons of new stores have opened and the face of retail has changed dramatically. I know things are blooming all over the region.

It's my bet that just like the French, the British, and the Native Americans before you, you've come to New England for the specialty items. You're here for the combination of historical perspective and souvenir collecting. Even if you didn't push your canoe upstream to trade a few pelts, I assume you're looking for a touch of the Old World or the colonial world mixed in with your clapboard houses and your blueberry pie.

What you get in today's New England is a New-World blend. I'm going to tell you about sugaring and maple syrup, about crafts and antiques and tag sales—but I'm also going to tell you about saving money and factory outlets. I'm going to send you home with a coffee mug shaped like a lobster, a T-shirt from the bar that inspired the TV show "Cheers," and designer clothes bought at a fraction of their true cost at **Filene's Basement's** newest discount source, **The Vault.** (Where I bought, among other things, Ferragamo shoes for $69 a pair!)

If you've come to New England from overseas, I welcome you to the total picture: American history and history-making bargains in New England's outlet malls, villages, and garages. Just wait till you take in your first tag sale!

New England has been hard hit by the recession years. Don't be shocked by the empty storefronts you see. (But do be on the lookout for closeout sales.) There's recovery in the air and many new faces, but you'll still find some depressed areas. Don't give up hope.

NEW ENGLAND INFO

- Connecticut Tourist Office, 210 Washington St., Hartford, CT 06160, ☎ 800/282-6863; web site: **http://www.state.ct.us**
- Rhode Island Tourism, 7 Jackson Walkway, Providence, RI 02903, ☎ 800/556-2484; web site: **http://www.visitrhodeisland.com**

- Massachusetts Tourism Office, 100 Cambridge St., Boston, MA 02202, ☎ 800/447-6277; web site: http://www.mass-vacation.com
- Vermont Travel Division, 134 State St., Montpelier, VT 05602, ☎ 802/828-3236; web site: http://www.travel-vermont.com
- New Hampshire Office of Vacation Travel, 105 Loudon Rd., Concord, NH 03301, ☎ 800/234-2300; web site: http://www.visitnh.gov
- Maine Publicity Bureau, 97 Winthrop St., Hallowell, ME 04347, ☎ 800/344-9948; web site: http://www.state.me.us/decd/tour

ELECTRONICALLY YOURS

Web Sites

http://www.discovernewengland.com   Joint marketing venture by all six states with tons of info including stuff from *Yankee* magazine.

http://www.magnet.state.ma.us/travel/travel.html   The great state of Massachusetts online.

http://www.bostonmagazine.com   *Boston* magazine on-line.

AUTOMOBILE-ASSOCIATION DEALS

Another great source of free information—and sizable savings—is your local AAA office. If you aren't a member of the Automobile Association of America, you may find it pays to join prior to a trip to New England just because of the benefits. And we don't mean flat-tire and tow-truck benefits; AAA tries to save you from flat wallets.

We received free maps, free tour books, discount coupons for car rental, and a trusty TripTik™. There are also AAA discounts available for theme parks and other attractions. In fact, wherever we go, we now ask if there is an AAA discount. When your hotel rate drops from $125 to $105 right before your eyes, you'll be as impressed as we were.

And your membership has added international benefits—like AmEx traveler's checks without a fee—so don't think of this as a New England–only kind of deal.

ATTENTION FOREIGN VISITORS

· ·

With airfares to and from Boston so accessible, Canada's borders just a short drive away, and America's seemingly reasonable prices (when compared to those in Europe), more and more Canadian and European travelers are visiting the U.S. Whether you're here on business or holiday, I just know you'll do some shopping.

- We do not have VAT (Value-Added Tax) in this country; each state has a different taxation policy and taxes goods at a different rate.
- Sales tax is added to the bill at the time of purchase, so the ticket price is not the final price you pay. Even if you take the merchandise out of the U.S., there is no refund on state tax. Sorry.
- Before these tax facts depress you, consider that the highest sales tax in the U.S. is less than half of the VAT. New Hampshire has no sales tax; Massachusetts has no sales tax on clothing under $79. Connecticut has no tax on clothing items under $50 each.
- Postal rates in the U.S. are quite reasonable if you're planning on shipping your goods home. Ask at the post office for rates for both airmail and surface mail. On the customs receipt mark the item a gift with a value of less than $25. Expect to pay duty on high-ticket items; make sure you're familiar with your laws.
- Purchase Protection is an international plan offered by American Express. Anything you buy in

the U.S. gets a free and automatic 90-day insurance policy when charged on your AmEx card.
- Your credit and bank card companies will convert purchases made in dollars to your home currency automatically at the time you are billed, giving you the best possible rate of exchange. Use plastic for most purchases to get easy-to-check records.

NEW ENGLAND GUIDES

. . . .

My best guides were the free AAA books, the free local handouts that you get in every town (they have paid listings, but are also filled with coupons), and two magazine-style guidebooks that are so similar we think you'd be happy with either: *Yankee Magazine's Travel Guide to New England* or *The Original New England Guide*. Each is published annually and costs about $5.

If copies are not available at newsstands in your area, write to: *The Original New England Guide*, New England Lifestyle Publications, Inc., 177 E. Industrial Dr., Manchester, NH 03103; or Yankee Publishing Inc., 3 S. Sixth St., New Bedford, MA 02710. Many guides to New England may also include information on parts of New York State and Canada.

Since part of the New England ethic places a high value on the printed word, you will find marvelous bookstores (especially in Boston and Cambridge) and many local magazines to which you can subscribe.

Boston has its own city magazine (*Boston*, natch), while almost every state has at least one statewide magazine. There are also country lifestyle magazines that feature the New England lifestyle. Almost all of these guides have coupon programs, so for the purchase price of a magazine, you may save money on some aspects of your visit.

Also note that once a year *Boston* magazine publishes its own list of the best things in town, which is considered the local version of a Michelin star by some.

SLEEPING NEW ENGLAND

. . . .

Part of the fantasy of New England is the dream of a small inn or bed-and-breakfast. Watch out! Throughout the research for this book, we became so disenchanted with B&B's that I now offer Gershman's Law of Sleeping New England: Go with a major chain that promises a certain standard—especially if you are with children or people who don't like to take chances.

When I want a known quantity in New England, I usually go for either Sheraton or Hilton (and I know their toll-free numbers by heart). ITT Sheraton is headquartered in Boston and thus has hotels throughout New England. They may not be small, quaint, or romantic, but especially if you are traveling with kids, they are probably your best bet for size and modern convenience.

There are Hiltons and Ramadas and Marriotts in many locations, but if you want to do one-stop booking and make it simple, you'll go with Sheraton. They have a SureSaver plan for discounts; Sheraton doesn't own a lot of these hotels, they just manage them or franchise some of them—so quality will vary. Call 800/325-3535 to have ITT Sheraton send you their directory of hotels. While this is an international guide, it tells you everything you need to know about New England on a state-by-state basis, complete with a picture of each hotel and directions for getting there. Since you will most likely be driving, this is invaluable information. The same toll-free number will take your reservation and provide you with updates on special promotions and rates.

Hotel Chains in New England

DAYS INN   There are almost 60 hotels in the New England area with prices ranging from $29 to $69 per night in their "New England Rates" package. The hotel we saw in Bridgeport, Connecticut, was a modern high-rise; the one we stayed at in Brimfield, Massachusetts, was a motel affair that offered a room at a great price, considering we were there for a flea market. In the U.S. call 800/325-2525 for reservations.

HILTON   There aren't as many Hiltons in New England as would be nice, but they have a well-located Boston Back Bay property and the best hotel in Mystic, Connecticut. There are sometimes promotional deals, although we've always found those rates sold out. We've paid slightly over $100 per night per double room. Boston costs more, of course. In the U.S. call 800/HILTONS for reservations and information.

HOWARD JOHNSON   There are about 40 properties in New England, and while we don't count on HoJo the way we did on all those family driving trips in the 1960s, they're out there and offer clean rooms and fair prices. Good location on the Mystic, Connecticut, property. Call 800/654-2000 in the U.S. for reservations.

MARRIOTT   With about 15 hotels in the New England area, and tons of promotional deals, Marriott may offer the hotel or resort of your dreams. Certainly their Newport, Rhode Island, property has set the town on its ear; their Boston harbor-front hotel wins accolades constantly. Prices can vary enormously from location to location. In the U.S. call 800/USA-WKND.

RAMADA INN   We didn't see a lot of Ramada Inns while we were on the road, and the one we did stay at was nothing to write home about, but that discount coupon in the AAA book made us grin with glee. Our double room, which had been confirmed at a rate of $64, went down to under $50 per night.

Who needs charm with prices like that? Call 800/
228-2828 for reservations.

SHERATON   Corporate offices in Boston and
hotels, be they Tara brand or plain old Sheraton,
are dotted everywhere. Even in Hartford, Connecticut, we found Sheraton a winner. Call 800/
325-3535.

Corporate Rates

Last time I called Sheraton to book a room I was
offered an assortment of rates, including a corporate rate of $104, which is about $20 less than the
next rate. Then they asked for my corporation, so I
said Simon & Schuster/Viacom—owners of my publishing company. It worked! So next time you're
booking rates, be my guest.

P.S. I later saw a discount coupon offered for this
hotel that would have brought the rate down to $99,
which just goes to show you that no matter how
many tricks you think you know, sometimes you
can't beat the system.

About Country Inns

If we knew how to pick a great inn from a blind
point of view, we'd be sure to tell you. We've gone
by the guidebooks, by the ads, and by the infamous
wander-around-town method. Our greatest dis-
appointments and outright disasters came from
fabulous write-ups in guidebooks we had respected
up until the point of check-in . . . or shortly there-
after.

We also had the crazy experience of getting two
recommendations from the chamber of commerce
in one city and discovering that neither of these
places was listed in any of the half-dozen guidebooks
we were using. When it comes to small hotels, you
are your own best guidebook.

As consumers, we have a few other caveats about
inns to pass along: Many of the best inns—the

fanciest ones, anyway—do not welcome children. Some say outright "no children" or "no children under 12." Ask!

Many old homes that have been turned into inns rarely have the space and amenities that hotel chains offer. You may find a sofa bed in a junior suite in a few inns; you probably will not find two double beds in one room.

Inns may also offer you a choice of prices based on the inclusion of dinner. In many cases an inn will be in the boonies and going out for dinner can be a major enterprise—you may do better to buy the dinner-inclusive package. If you have children with you, the dining experience in a dinner-included stay may be far too fancy and a total waste of money. Ask a lot of questions and know your family's eating habits before you plunge in.

You may want to look at a book called *Innkeeper's Register,* dated by the year, which gives pointers on specific B&B's. Call 800/344-5244.

While I adore looking through the scads of B&B and country-inn books and magazines at every bookstore and newsstand, I know that many of these guides take paid listings, which makes me doubt the reliability of the write-up. I also believe that a picture is indeed worth a thousand words; try to book places that have sent you a brochure with *several* photos.

GETTING THERE

. . . .

Boston is considered the transportation hub of New England, but you can explore a variety of New England treats without using Boston as your base. If you're out to impress your neighbors and business buddies with just how plugged in you are, you may have already begun to use the Providence, Rhode Island, airport. In fact, a new revolutionary war has been fought in New England in the past few years over airlines and no-frills (oops, Yankee Thrift) airfares. Now Southwest Airlines uses Providence as its New England hub. Read on!

By Plane

Boston may have the most flights and therefore the best promotion prices, but if you are having trouble getting the deal or the date you want, try the **Providence** airport, T. F. Green International. (Note that although it's called the Providence airport, it's actually located in Warwick.) It's an hour from Boston, equidistant to the Cape, and provides easy access to coastal New England. Considering the savings to be had by booking with a no-frills carrier, you can start to understand the additional lure of Rhode Island. I happened to notice that one of the Kennedy boys is a state senator or a congressman from the state of Rhode Island. It just goes to show that when Massachusetts gets too small, everyone heads for Rhode Island!

If you don't mind small airplanes, you'll find service to all parts of New England and relatively easy access to airports you may never have heard of before. I have more specifics on travel directly to Boston in Chapter 8, page 141.

By Train

Amtrak services New England with three different routes: north from New York toward Canada, east from New York along the coast to Boston, and east from Albany, New York. In the summer there is train/ bus service to the Cape. Call 800/USA-RAIL for information and reservations.

Amtrak prices are reasonable, especially when you're taking along the kids—but the trains do have their problems. We've had wonderful, smooth trips and we've been stuck in stations for hours of delays caused by breakdowns. Europeans may be appalled by the state of the American train system, but since it's all we've got, we bring a book and sit back for the ride.

Amtrak sells a limited number of first-class seats that are about twice the price of regular seats, but the added cost does get you a plush compartment and a reserved seat. (Trains can often be so packed that you are lucky to get standing room.)

If you are traveling to Boston by train, call the hotel and ask at which train station you should alight. Several leading hotels in Boston are far closer to the Back Bay Station, so there is no reason to take the train all the way to South Station. Other cities also have suburban stations, so be sure to ask.

Don't be surprised if some of your train trip ends up on a bus. Tracks are poor or nonexistent in some areas, so bus links are needed.

By Bus

Bus service, other than that provided by Amtrak, is available and particularly well organized: There are point-to-point trips, day trips, or complete tours. Even if you disdain the thought of bus travel in real life, it's a smart choice for seeing New England because you get to enjoy the views without the driving, and short hops are the rule.

AAA offers bus plans and tours; there are many independent bus deals in the Boston area as well. There are bus trips for New Yorkers for special doings such as big antiques fairs or crafts events.

Among the bus companies with service into and around New England: **Bonanza** (☎ 800/556-3815); **Greyhound** (☎ 800/231-2222); **Concord Trailways** (☎ 617/426-8080); **Peter Pan Trailways** (☎ 800/237-8747); and **Vermont Transit Lines** (☎ 800/451-3292).

By Car

Car-rental promotions are plentiful; check rates and deals before you sign up. Remember, location of rental offices counts. There are no car-rental offices inside the Boston South Station train station, nor are there any at the Route 128 station. *But,* there are offices of about a million competing companies around the Back Bay Station area.

Being open counts, at least to me.

I got to our appointed rental office in Boston on Sunday and found it closed. We had to pay for two taxi rides. (And have psychiatric care to recover from the stress!) The rental office may reimburse you for the cab ride to their offices, but they will not pay for round-trip cabs. Be sure to ask; they won't volunteer.

Some rental agencies in New England have a new program whereby you sign up for a gas replenishment fee. You pay an additional fee up front (about $10) and then return the car with the tank empty, or nearly empty. You'll be charged to refill the tank, but at the going gasoline rate—not the ridiculously exorbitant car-rental gasoline rate that is usually charged. It comes out about the same, but may save you time if you're in a hurry. Ask for details.

If you rent your car on one of the islands, you may get a discount by mentioning a promotional coupon at the time of rental. Ask!

By Ferry

If you are traveling by ferry to Martha's Vineyard or Nantucket, there is much to learn, especially about getting reservations for your car, getting tickets, and even choosing parking lots. For example, if you buy an advance-purchase ticket for a person (not a car) through your travel agent, you will pay a fee (about $3 per ticket) and you will still have to arrive in time to pick up the ticket. (So the fee isn't for mail charges.)

But if you buy the ticket at the ferry-terminal ticket window, there's no fee. If you get any of the many freebie guides to Cape Cod, you'll notice there may be coupons that will entitle you to a $2.50 or $3 discount on each adult ticket! We are not saying to hold out until the last minute, however, because you could end up in hot water. (Or very, very cold water.)

Ferry firms have been experimenting with different policies, especially on reservations and preordering tix, so call around for information as soon as you plan your trip. Don't wait for the last minute!

Among the firms with ferry service to the islands are **Hy-Line** (☎ 508/778-2600), **Island Queen** (☎ 508/548-4800), the state-run **Steamship Authority** (☎ 508/477-8600), and **Cape Island Express** (☎ 508/997-1688). Note that **Bay State Cruises** (☎ 617/723-7800 or 508/487-9274) has round-trip service between Boston and Provincetown.

By Cruise

Several leading firms now offer cruises to New England that usually include some part of Canada. These may be round-trip from New York, or one-way from Canada to New York, or vice versa. None of the big lines is currently operating out of Boston, though you can get tour boats and ferries in Boston.

While the cruise lines cover a lot of territory, none of them calls in Boston at all. You're more likely to disembark at smaller New England ports, some in Nova Scotia, and then at stops deeper in Canada along the St. Lawrence River.

PHONING AROUND

Like all other parts of America, New England has had to expand its telephone area codes in order to create more lines. Hence, many states have new codes but printed materials may have old codes. Remember, patience is a Yankee virtue!

Chapter Three

· · · · · · · ·

SHOPPING STRATEGIES

IN-SEASON SHOPPING

· ·

If you are looking to save on room rates or house rentals, try to plan your trip to coincide with a nonpeak season. For instance, we were offered a house in Nantucket that costs $1,500 a week in season (June, July, August) or $300 a week out of season. And that included time in April and parts of May. There are a number of Thanksgiving and Christmas promotional deals, especially in Boston, in bigger country inns, and in colonial villages. Do remember that winter may be considered off-season in coastal areas of New England, but it is "in season" at ski areas, and prices can be high.

Shopping prices also have a seasonal edge to them; antiques dealers will not bargain in the summer. Ski clothing is least expensive in the summer, and so on. Opposites attract all right—opposite seasons should attract smart shoppers who are looking ahead.

PICK-YOUR-OWN SHOPPING

· ·

The fact that New England has distinct seasons is part of its attraction. Each season brings its own shopping trends. Locals always know their produce by the time of year; they can tell you the week when Silver Queen corn is harvested. Farm stands are abundant and yummy to look at. Some are quite commercial, others so authentic you may want to whip out your camera. Stands usually open by Memorial Day Weekend, but may not be fully stocked until around July 4, depending on sun, rain, and growing conditions. Most stay open until the end of October to usher in the apple, cider, and pumpkin season.

Aside from the stands themselves, you'll find many fields ripe for the picking. Picking produce is actually a major tourist sport. We will never get over the ethereal experience of picking strawberries on a ridge overlooking Narragansett Bay. We've picked our way across Connecticut, Rhode Island, and southern New Hampshire and suggest it as a way to find bargains and fun and to get some fruit and vegetables into your kids.

There are some 60 farms in Connecticut alone that invite guests to pick-their-own; for a listing write for their free booklet, but enclose a stamped, self-addressed envelope: **Connecticut Dept. of Agriculture,** 165 Capitol Ave. #263, Hartford, CT 06106.

Farmer's Markets

Country fresh produce is part of the New England fantasy . . . and reality. More and more farmer's markets are popping up in cities where a farm stand might not normally be part of your day. To get a list of the markets in any given city or state, write that state's Department of Agriculture.

CAMPUS SHOPPING

Most university campuses are not in downtown commercial districts; some have direct access to "real-world" shopping, others are so isolated that students are forced to shop on campus and pay full retail. For tourists who want university souvenirs, especially Ivy League items, the local "coop" or bookstore should have what you want. A large number of university bookstores in America are run on a cooperative basis. Students are members of the co-op, provide a number when they shop, or save their receipts, and receive a cash dividend at the end of the school year. In usual circumstances the co-op is called a "co-op" (as in co-operative), but in Cambridge, the Harvard and MIT co-ops are known as "coops" (as in chicken).

University-imprinted merchandise is big business, especially for a handful of New England Ivys. Don't be surprised if you see different merchandise in discount stores than what you'd find in the coops. Often these goods are made by more than one company and the licenses are sold for separate areas of retail. Many of the universities have catalogs and mail-order divisions.

MUSEUM SHOPPING

New England is famous for its museums, especially its specialty museums. Each has its own gift shop or gift counter. Some have catalogs and mail-order plans. Your best opportunity for finding unique and affordable gifts (and souvenirs) lies in the museum store for the region. The store in the Boston Museum of Fine Arts is overrated, but its catalog is one of the best in the world. For great shops, check out Mystic, Deerfield, and Sturbridge Village.

SHAKER SHOPPING

Various Shaker communities in New England have gift shops. The goods are usually reproduction Shaker. Antique Shaker goods are expensive and highly prized. Many of the Shaker communities in

New Hampshire, Vermont, and Massachusetts are open as tourist attractions and educational facilities, allowing you to peer into a way of life that is just about gone forever. Shaker products represent a quality of workmanship that cannot be duplicated in modern production. Shakers are famous for their wood furniture, but also for the invention of the pincushion, the broom, the clothes pin, and the marketing of garden seed. You can still buy seed in most Shaker gift shops.

ROOTS SHOPPING

Since New England has been the port of entry for generations of immigrants, tracing one's roots is a popular pastime. If you are doing this research as part of your vacation, come to New England prepared. Gather whatever family information you already have, including oral or written tidbits. Look for legally recorded dates as the opening of secrets—when were family members born or married? When and where did they die? Military records can also be helpful; religious records may prove more helpful. If you plan to use local facilities, call ahead to make sure that they have what you need, will be open when you plan to visit, and will be able to help you. Ask if there is a fee for you to use their records. Contact historical societies; make use of state libraries, state archives, church records, university records, and cemetery records.

Use published genealogies if you know your family had a footing in a particular state or area. Yankee Books (Camden, Maine) publishes a book called *Shaking Your Family Tree*, available in many New England bookstores, which gives you step-by-step directions for finding your Yankee roots. Not only does it have invaluable information and much explanation, but there are charts and appendices of information essential for mastering the materials available.

SKI SHOPPING

All the ski resorts have two types of retail: sports-related and tourist-related. You are encouraged to buy your ski needs in situ and then to shop when you aren't schussing down the slopes. Many ski communities have adorable shopping districts. They also have pretty adorable sales at the end of the ski season.

SUGAR SHOPPING

Sugaring is the process by which maple trees are tapped and sap is collected. The sap is boiled down in a long (and often tedious) process and eventually becomes maple syrup. The sugaring process is a New England ritual that signifies the end of winter (most sugaring takes place in March) and celebrates the sweetness of life. To be part of the process, look for farms that allow you to tag along. For a list of Vermont sugar houses, write the **Vermont Department of Agriculture,** 116 State St., Montpelier, VT 06602, or call 802/828-2500. You can also contact: **Bacon's Sugar House,** Jaffrey Center, NH (☎ 603/532-8836); **Barretts's Sugar House,** Keene, NH (☎ 603/357-0903); or **Harlow's Sugar House,** Putney, VT (☎ 802/387-5852).

WHALE SHOPPING

OK, so you can't really buy a whale . . . but you can adopt one. The adoption fee is $15, although you are encouraged to give $25. When you adopt, you get an adoption certificate with your name and the name of the adoptee, a photo of your whale, a whale calendar, a quarterly newsletter, and a card for discounts on whale-watch expeditions on Cape Cod. Write to: Whale Adoption Project, International Wildlife Coalition, 634 N. Falmouth Hwy., P.O.

Box 388, North Falmouth, MA 02556. You can also call 508/564-9980. You can order by phone with a credit card.

STOVE SHOPPING

Perhaps the most lasting souvenir you'll bring home from your trip is the memory of life in front of the fireplace. The old-fashioned stove seems to be part of the New England lifestyle. While you can buy an old stove at various antiques fairs, markets, or dealers, if you'd like a new version of an old-fashioned stove shipped to you anyplace in the U.S., consider contacting Vermont Castings at ☎ 800/227-8683 for a variety of stove styles that can be installed without chimneys. Or if you prefer, Woodstock Soapstone Co. (☎ 800/866-4344) sells old-fashioned, four-legged soapstone stoves.

COUNTRY-STORE SHOPPING

Rural New England has its own version of the convenience store: the country store. These general stores offer a little of everything—one-stop shopping for locals and a possible sightseeing and shopping adventure for visitors. Most country stores sell dry goods, home-baked goods, fresh and frozen foodstuffs, wood, magazines, etc. Some even offer video rental. The reason to go to these stores is not to see what they sell or to do any serious shopping, but to soak up a way of retail that is quickly fading from the fabric of American life. The country store is at least a hundred years old in its current form and really has its roots in the precolonial trading post. The mall was never like this!

LIQUOR SHOPPING

. . . .

Not to end this litany of retail charms on the wrong note, but for those who are big drinkers, you should probably be aware that there are different consumer laws and different price policies in the various New England states. There's also been a problem around certain state borders and across the U.S.-Canada border with people running booze. Al Capone, where are you now?

Locals are well aware that liquor is about 25% to 30% less expensive in New Hampshire than in Massachusetts; they often drive some distance to stock up. Because so many people buy booze in New Hampshire, the state has no sales tax and no state personal income tax!

Chapter Four

· · · · · · ·

FACTORY OUTLETS

WELCOME TO THE OUTLETS

· ·

New England has more factory outlets than any other region of the U.S. The outlet business has become so sophisticated in the last decade that entire cities are now devoted solely to outlet shopping, and have a multitiered system of outlets.

There are real factory outlets (they are in the factories), there are fake factory outlets (they just say they are outlets), there are manufacturers' factory stores (next best thing to being in the factory), and there are jobbers, off-pricers, and outleteers who go by their own name, who buy from many sources and sell at discounted prices. The best way to get a handle on all of this is to shop, shop, shop and see what works for you.

In my shopping around, I've found that the manufacturers who have gone heavily into the factory store system are opening cookie-cutter branch stores in outlet-mall developments all over the country. Seen one, you've seen them all. So we thought the best service we could provide you with would be a list of the basic players and a rundown of what they usually carry in their typical outlet store. Quality of merchandise will vary to some extent in different locations, but for people who have the choice of many outlet malls, it can be helpful to have this scorecard before heading out.

Please note that the outlet business is the most positive part of the retail scene in the U.S. these days. It's growing steadily; new malls may have opened since we've gone to press, new makers may have joined the game, stores may have moved within a city. When you get to town, get a mall directory for an up-to-the-minute report from the landlords.

THE OUTLET BIZ

· ·

It gives me a warm, cozy feeling to think that New England is dotted with hundreds (maybe thousands) of deserted mills and factories; that these spaces can be/have been/will be revitalized and turned into retail centers and/or factory outlets. Casting the glow aside, the truth is that outlets are a gigantic business and one of the few aspects of American retail business that is flourishing. While makers used to use their closed-down mills for factory stores, and you can still find a real factory with a real outlet store (like the American Tourister Factory in Warren, Rhode Island), chances are that the outlets in which you will be shopping are part of the new scene. They were put there just for tourists.

Granted, outlet stores and malls are rarely in big cities, since manufacturers want no conflict with their regular accounts. But New England is dotted with entire communities that echo with the sound of cash registers ringing.

The demographics of the outlet shopper prove that he or she comes from a family where the annual income is in the $55,000-to-$75,000 range; the shopper has a craving for the best, but wants it at a discount. To get the goods, shoppers have proven they will drive up to 90 minutes from their home town. Or they'll schedule a vacation holiday in an area around an existing outlet mall—they will leave the beaten tourist path to shop for a day. International visitors are even more enthusiastic.

ATTENTION INTERNATIONAL SHOPPERS

If you come from England or Europe you have probably noticed that regular retail prices in the U.S. are half of what they are at home; that everything seems like a bargain. When you get to an outlet, expect savings of 25% to 75% off American retail prices. Most New England outlets will ship to Canada, some will ship to the United Kingdom and Europe. Most take plastic; all take traveler's checks. You do not get a VAT refund on state tax, sorry. Some states, however, do not charge tax. You will pay duty on goods sent home; mark them carefully. If you mail yourself packages, mark them as gifts valued under $25.

BOOKING OUTLETS

Outlet Bound is a booklet listing outlets all over the country, organized by region. I bought my copy in the magazine section of my local bookstore, but you can call 800/336-8853 to order directly from the publisher, or write to: Outlet Bound, P.O. Box 1255, Orange, CT 06477.

Outlet Shopper's Guide is published by the group that produces New York's *S&B Report* (sales and bargains) with national listings for outlets all over the country. It's available through mail order only, for $9.95. Write to the Lazar Media Group, 112 E. 36th St., 4th Floor, New York, NY 10016.

DEPARTMENT-STORE OUTLETS

Department stores have finally seen the light and joined the team, creating clearance centers where unsold floor merchandise can be unloaded at discount.

Filene's Basement is no longer the outlet for the Filene's department store, so don't let this throw you.

Technically speaking, **The Basement** is an off-pricer, not a department-store outlet. They have more than 50 branch stores springing up all over the U.S.— with a high concentration in New England since the mother ship is in Boston.

Department-store outlet stores are still limited in number and are not particularly plentiful in New England, but a few are gaining ground. Macy's now has nine outlet stores (called **Close-Out**) in the U.S., including a relatively new one in Holyoke, Massachusetts. Saks now has a few of their outlets, **Off Fifth,** in New England, with more coming on a regular basis. This is the hottest department-store outlet in terms of growth and sales. There's one in Worcester, Massachusetts, and one in Clinton, Connecticut.

DEFINITIONS FIRST

. . . .

FACTORY STORE   The factory store is in the factory, like the **Reebok** outlet store in the Reebok factory in Stoughton, Massachusetts. Often the factory store is just open to employees, so word doesn't get around. Sometimes the factory store is open to the public once a year (like **Dooney & Bourke** in Norwalk, Connecticut). Sometimes there's a small factory store but once or twice a year they have a blowout sale (like **C. R. Gibson** in Norwalk, Connecticut). A factory store is always on the factory grounds.

FACTORY-OWNED STORE   Sometimes the factory leases retail space, usually in an outlet mall, for their outlet store. Prices are usually the same as in the factory store (in the factory), but there may not be the same selection. Generally speaking, the factory store in the factory has the best selection and the outlet stores all have the same kind of selection— merchandise has been divvied up accordingly. Still, it's a great way to save money.

OFF-PRICER   A store that buys goods from many makers and factories and sells them at less than regular retail, but at more than the factory-outlet price (sometimes less, in the case of a closeout). Off-price chains include **Loehmann's, Marshalls, Hit or Miss, Dress Barn, T. J. Maxx,** etc. There are also some off-pricers in the outlet malls. You probably will not recognize their names.

MANUFACTURERS OUTLET DIRECTORY

The following directory does not begin to cover all the manufacturers who have gone into the outlet business or who have outlet stores in New England. It is merely a list of our favorites, those that keep popping up with frequency, and those that we've never heard of and investigated for academic purposes. This directory works on the assumption that the outlet stores are more or less the same. Amount of stock and sizes available will, of course, vary from outlet to outlet; usually available styles do not vary that much.

We also list the New England cities where you'll find these stores. The best way to know exactly what is where is to pick up the locally published (free) guide at each mall city. Our listings are meant to give you the basic idea, but may not be the final word as the factory-outlet scene continues to grow. Small strip and freestanding outlets are not included in these listings.

Adolfo

Well, it's not exactly Nancy Reagan time. This is a licensed brand of inexpensive-to-moderately priced clothes from the very famous Adolfo himself. Comparing this line to his real collection is somewhat difficult since there are very few similarities between a $2,000 suit and a $100 one. With that understanding, the outlet stores sell a selection of mostly knit goods, usually offered as separates. Many of the Chanel-inspired styles work well in this price range, and you can put together a skirt-and-sweater suit at the outlet for not much more than $100. Note, for the sticklers in the crowd, Adolfo was out of business for many years. About two years ago he very quietly went back into business with Saks Fifth Avenue on an exclusive basis and now makes The Suit again. I've seen some at Loehmann's, so don't get confused between the good stuff, which might pop up at an off-pricer, and what you see at these outlets. Not that you would be confused.

Store locations: Bourne, MA; Lenox, MA

Etienne Aigner

Etienne Aigner is a big name in Europe, but not so well known in America. The firm is famous for its leather goods (shoes and handbags) and has a little logo of an *A* with a horseshoe on it that is recognized as a symbol of quality and status. The goods are indeed well made and pricey. This is one of the higher-end lines to be carried in an outlet situation. There are also clothes (mostly sportswear), men's belts, and leather accessories. The look is sort of the rich Italian horse-breeder type.

Store location: Kittery, ME

American Tourister

One of the most prolific companies in the outlet business, American Tourister stores usually offer a wide range of styles at discount, some backpacks, carry-ons, briefcases, wallets, and travel supplies. Most of the styles are arranged by complete set so you can see all the matching pieces. There are usually two racks filled with unmatched pieces that have been further marked down. These pieces are discontinued, so you may not be able to put together a matching three- or four-piece set. You can easily buy a large Pullman suitcase on wheels for $40 to $50.

The factory itself is halfway between Providence and Newport, Rhode Island.

Store locations: Branford, CT; Westbrook, CT; North Dartmouth, MA; Kittery, ME; North Conway, NH; North Hampton, NH

LAURA ASHLEY

There are not a huge number of Laura Ashley outlets; the ones we've been to have been dramatically different from each other. For the most part, the stores are only modestly decorated in the Ashley mode. Don't be surprised if some merchandise is displayed right in the cartons. The ready-to-wear is usually a season old, but merchandise can be several years old when it comes to fabrics and decorating needs. This doesn't really matter since most Ashley is considered a classic of its type. The best buys are on wallpaper and fabric by the yard. Wallpaper is sold in a European measure, which means that one roll of Laura Ashley wallpaper is equal to almost two rolls of any American brand. If you are buying wallpaper, know your measurements so you can buy the right amount.

Store location: Freeport, ME

BALLY

Swiss shoe and leather firm with absolutely gorgeous outlet stores where prices are actually affordable. Tons of shoes for men and women as well as handbags, business accessories, leather clothing, and to-die-for luxury goods.

Store location: Worcester, MA

BANANA REPUBLIC

Well, the truth is that we love these clothes; we love the retail shops and visit them regularly. But the outlet? C'mon, who really buys this stuff? Prices are not much better than regular in-store markdowns and this stuff looks a bit worn. Despite the large, attractive interior, we are not able to rave about this outlet.

Note: I have seen some Banana Republic merchandise and toiletries at Gap Outlets in malls in New England—even in the downtown Boston outlet, which is not in a mall.

Store locations: North Conway, NH; Freeport, ME

BANNISTER SHOE

Now they have several brands in this outlet, including some Nine West; several shoe lines at several different price points. Very promotion-oriented.

Store locations: Clinton, CT; Mystic, CT; Freeport, ME; Kittery, ME

BARBIZON

Outlets are usually medium-sized but well stocked with sleepwear. There are always many styles, including a selection of beautiful flannel gowns, which are not as grandmotherly as you might expect. No matter what time of year you shop there will be sleepwear for other seasons, although the main body of the stock is seasonal. A great place for gifts.

Store locations: Bourne, MA; Freeport, ME; North Conway, NH

BASS

Bass is famous for shoes, but they also make handbags, tote bags, and small leather goods. They are most famous for their penny-loafer styles, but also make sports shoes for men and women.

Store locations: Clinton, CT; Mystic, CT; Worcester, MA; Freeport, ME; Kittery, ME; North Hampton, NH; Manchester, VT

EDDIE BAUER

It's pretty hard to tell the Eddie Bauer look from the L. L. Bean look or the Orvis look. We've only been to one outlet store but it was well stocked. Bauer has stores in most big American malls and a huge catalog business—the outlet sells exactly what you see in the stores. About 35% of the store space is devoted to footgear, the rest is half men's clothing and half women's—although this look has a wide unisex range. Prices are definitely below regular retail; some featured items offer incredible savings.

There happens to be an Eddie Bauer outlet, a freestanding store no less, right smack dab in the middle of downtown Boston.

Store location: North Conway, NH

BCBG

Although this might be considered a French line because BCBG is a French expression (*bon chic bon genre*), this is actually a California line that is hip to the core and great for those who want to look cutting-edge without going over the top.

Store location: Clinton, CT

L. L. BEAN

There are three outlet stores as we go to press; we've been to two of them. There is one near Augusta, Maine, that we haven't made it to yet. The outlet in North Conway is large, has two levels, and offers discounts on anything you might need. The store in Freeport is about the same size, but seems to have a faster pace. Both stores offer a color-coded sales ticket discount system that greatly reduces the ticketed price at the cash register. Ask a lot of questions, because your first impression in one of these stores might be "Ye gads, these prices are high!" Note that the mother store and outlet store in Freeport are two different beasts.

Store locations: Augusta, ME; Freeport, ME; North Conway, NH

HARVE BENARD

There are many Benard outlets; they pop up everywhere—even at nonfamous outlet malls and strip centers. The merchandise is pretty much the same from one outlet to the next: women's career clothes, some women's accessories, shoes, and handbags. There is also a men's section. During some seasons, there are coats and raincoats.

Harve Benard clothes are not inexpensive, but they are of good quality and tailored to be fashionable in a classic way. At certain promotional times, they take an additional 20% or more off the outlet price. An excellent source for business clothes.

Store locations: East Norwalk, CT; Milford, CT; Lenox, MA; Freeport, ME; Keene, NH

BENETTON

Mixed reviews for Benetton outlet stores: I often sigh, "At last this merchandise has the right price tags." Prices are moderate to low; a few things are steals. Many seasons' worth of clothes can be hung together; you won't always find coordinating pieces. The kids' clothing is a standout.

Store locations: Worcester, MA; Freeport, ME; North Conway, NH; Manchester, VT

BLACK & DECKER

My husband Mike's favorite outlet. We admit we've only seen one of these hot spots in our travels, but one was enough. Park the men in the family for at least an hour, then stand back and try not to laugh when they come home loaded down with flashlights, electrical tools, leaf blowers, toasters, and more.

Store location: Kittery, ME

BOSTON TRADERS

High-end knitwear with a fashionably preppy edge; great use of design (often nautical) and color (brights for summer, earth tones for fall). While they make men's and women's clothing, the unisex sweaters are their bread and butter. Don't miss the kids' line either, sold at seperate shops.

Store locations: Freeport, ME; Kittery, ME; Manchester, VT

BOSTON TRADERS KIDS

Crafted with the same quality and care as the adult line, we think Boston Traders Kids is one of the best children's lines in America. Prices are high, even at the outlet, but if you hit a sale, you will have style and quality that is top-of-the-line. Sizes begin at infant and go up to size 20 for boys, 14 for girls.

Store locations: Norwalk, CT; Manchester, VT

BROOKS BROTHERS

We were shocked the first time we found an outlet store . . . even more shocked when we found out what was inside. The stores are nicely decorated, spacious, well lit, and stocked with men's and women's discounts and bargains. Some items— particularly men's suits—seem fairly priced without being called real bargains.

One shudders to think that people would pay much more for these clothes at regular retail. We saw men's dress shirts for $16; polo shirts with the Brooks Brothers logo were about $15. The colors were great and the size range good. Women's career clothes! Some kids' items. Filene's Basement may have better prices on BB during blowout sales, but not the same consistent selection.

Perhaps the award for buy of the century goes to my girlfriend Marie-Jo, who bought a black lace cocktail dress for $49!

Store locations: Clinton, CT; Freeport, ME; Kittery, ME; Manchester, VT

BROOKSTONE

Hmmm. Brookstone has a way to go before I'm impressed. Love the stores, but the outlets are, uh, boring. If this stuff is a bargain, then I'm Snow White. A few items did seem like good deals, but we weren't knocked out. Much of the stock is in damaged boxes and left over from catalog stock.

Brookstone retail stores are moderately priced and pleasant to shop. Their outlet may be a disappointment to anyone who really cares.

Store locations: Freeport, ME; North Conway, NH

BUGLE BOY

Attention mothers: Prices are fair, selection is gigantic. Bugle Boy outlets are almost warehouses with tons of merchandise in all sizes. The prices are no less than at your local Marshall's or off-pricer, but the choices are mind-boggling.

Store locations: East Norwalk, CT; Westbrook, CT; Kittery, ME; North Conway, NH

CAMBRIDGE DRY GOODS

One of our favorite lines for moderately priced clothing for men and women and—get this—they sell current stock in the outlet store. So you can really gloat over the deal you get when you pay 25% less for the exact same thing you can find at Bloomingdale's. The look is sort of updated preppy, not unlike the Boston Traders look.

Store locations: Freeport, ME; Kittery, ME

CAPE ISLE KNITTERS

Since I do not wear machine-made sweaters with cute little designs, I was not familiar with this line at retail. There are a fair number of outlet stores in New England, however, and women who like sweaters with counted-in designs of hearts or cats or snowflakes will find the quality is good.

Store locations: Mystic, CT; North Dartmouth, MA; Kittery, ME; North Conway, NH; North Hampton, NH

CARTER'S

Large, well-stocked shops with tons of things for kids, from newborn on up. Stock up on layette needs, basics, or fashion items. Great prices. Must-stop shopping for any mom-to-be or grandma. Baby Dior sold too.

Store locations: Cape Cod, MA; Fall River, MA; Freeport, ME; Kittery, ME

CHAMPION/HANES

Another division of Hanes, with the Champion sweats—mostly for men but many unisex.

Store locations: Mystic, CT; Westbrook, CT; Kittery, ME

CHUCK ROAST

This store specializes in rugged wear, mountain wear, and a country-western, outdoorsy look that works well with your L. L. Bean gear.

Store locations: Kittery, ME; North Conway, NH

LIZ CLAIBORNE

At the risk of being unpopular, I confess that Liz Claiborne outlets aren't cheap enough for me. The stores are usually large; they usually have a good selection of various sizes (including petites), handbags, and other items. There may or may not be a few pieces of Dana Buchman merchandise. Merchandise can be years old and not properly reduced. You can get a $50 dress for work.

Store locations: Clinton, CT; Bourne, MA; Freeport, ME; North Conway, NH; Manchester, VT

CLAIRE'S

Hmmm, I don't really think this is a true outlet even though there are stores in a number of outlet malls. Cheap accessories for teens.

Store location: Westbrook, CT

CLIFFORD & WILLS

Preppy.

Store location: Westbrook, CT

 ### COACH

Why these people have a retail business is beyond me. Once you've been in an outlet store, your life will change. Why pay retail? The stores are drop-dead chic, and the merchandise does not appear to be damaged at all. This is as good as it gets. Prices on these leather goods are 25% to 45% below retail; there are sales and promotions; men's and women's accessories and business gear.

Store locations: Clinton, CT; Freeport, ME; Manchester, VT

COLE-HAAN

Sneaky, sneaky, sneaky. Cole-Haan makes high-quality, statusy, preppy leather goods that look expensive because they are expensive. Their factory stores are carefully named because they sell factory-direct merchandise. That doesn't mean that they are outlet stores! Usually only one portion of the factory store is devoted to sale or discounted merchandise. Buyer beware!

Store locations: Clinton, CT; Freeport, ME; North Conway, NH; Manchester, VT

CONVERSE

If your kids are status-conscious (*if???*) and Converse—the brand with the big star—is a must-have, then you'll be thrilled to know that colored canvas sneakers can be found at the outlet store for about $10 a pair. There are many other types of shoes and even socks, but for us, those colored sneaks are the real draw.

Store locations: Fall River, MA; Worcester, MA; Kittery, ME; North Conway, NH

CORNING/REVERE

Excellent minisupermarket of cooking gadgets, inexpensive dishes, tabletop, and cookware, including the famous Paul Revere copper-bottom pots and pans. Great prices; great fun.

Store locations: Mystic, CT; Freeport, ME; North Hampton, NH

THE COSMETICS COMPANY

Do you love that for a name—*pullllease,* I would walk right by and forget it. But wait! These people are simply too proud to admit they have outlet stores now, a rather recent development in family history. In Lauder family history, that is. This is the Estee Lauder series of outlets; they carry perfumes and makeup and not everything but lots more than you expect and usually something from every branch in the family business including Origins, my favorite. Discounts are only 20% to 25%, so don't get carried away, but it's a little something.

Store locations: Clinton, CT; Kittery, ME

CRABTREE & EVELYN

If you thought this maker of soaps and creams was an old English company, stop the music. Although their packaging is very turn-of-the-century, the company was formed in the 1970s and it is American! Hence this outlet store with its own little secret: One side of the store sells at a discount, the other side is regular retail! Be careful, ask a lot of questions, and don't assume any bargains until you're sure. Then stock up!

Store location: Freeport, ME

CRATE & BARREL

The outlet looks as good as any of their regular retail shops; the discounts are on housewares, tablewares, and goodies you want to buy for yourself or give as gifts.

Store locations: Clinton, CT; Kittery, ME

J. CREW

I love J. Crew catalogs. I love J. Crew stores. I surely love J. Crew outlet stores. My only problem is that even at outlet prices, this stuff isn't cheap.

Watch for bargains and promotions; know the catalog price before you assume you are getting a deal. The stores are well designed and well stocked; the clothing is clean and bright and plentiful. Now only 40% of the total line is sold through the catalog so you may see new styles. Bridge clothing— work clothes just one step beneath designer prices— is the latest.

Store locations: Westbrook, CT; Freeport, ME; Kittery, ME

DANSK

Dansk has outlet stores in many established malls as well as in many out-of-the-way freestanding locations. Stores are large- to medium-sized and are pleasantly designed and easy to shop. All the merchandise is Dansk; prices are about 25% off retail, but there are often coupons or promotional postcards that offer extra savings. The enamel cookware is one of their staples. They ship. Note that this is a Danish-inspired and designed firm but an American company; there are no longer any Dansk stores in Scandinavia.

Store locations: Hyannis, MA; Worcester, MA; Kittery, ME; North Conway, NH

DANSKIN

Danskin is the leading name in dance and bodywear; their tights were fashionable before tights were "in." They have more size ranges than normal hosiery companies; their tights do not run as easily as other brands. Everything is discounted at the outlet; colors that are "out" are marked down even lower.

Store locations: Clinton, CT; North Conway, NH

DEXTER SHOE

Dexter is one of the oldest New England shoemakers still in business. They have outlets everyplace you look: some in malls, some freestanding. They offer a wide range of shoes for the whole family—although their specialty is sort of a rugged, preppy Yankee look.

Store locations: Freeport, ME; North Conway, NH

DOONEY & BOURKE

The Dooney & Bourke people used to work at Coach before going out on their own with this similar-but-different look. Both names are status symbols for Yankees and suburbanites all over. The Dooney & Bourke outlet business is not nearly as developed as Coach's, but you can get a good deal if you are lucky. The store in Freeport is as cute as a mall boutique and is well stocked with various colors and styles.

Because Dooney & Bourke is headquartered in Norwalk, they also sell at The Company Store in the East Norwalk Factory Outlet Mall. The selection here is not as deep as in an outlet store, but it is wider in choices (though limited in colors). You may also find returns here that sell for under $100.

Store locations: Clinton, CT; Freeport, ME

EPISODE

Hong Kong–based firm selling upscale sportswear that's far more fun when discounted.

Store location: Clinton, CT

FANNY FARMER

Don't eat too much, or you'll need to come back to the outlet malls for a wardrobe in a new size! Except for the seasonal goodies, we can't figure out where the discounted merchandise is.

Store location: North Conway, NH

LESLIE FAY

Leslie Fay offers a selection of casual, business, and dressy wear for women who want a fairly conservative look. They have large sizes and a pretty good selection of dressy clothes.

Store locations: Kittery, ME; North Hampton, NH

ESCADA/FIRST CHOICE

There's only one First Choice outlet in New England so far, but it's a goodie. That's because First Choice sells Escada, Laurel, and Crisca clothes from the German design team that creates all three. Also some accessories.

Store location: New Bedford, MA

GAP

The Gap has very slowly joined the outlet bandwagon. They have Old Navy stores all over the U.S., which is their official way of handling the outlet situation, but now there are a few outlets here and there.

I have only one word to share with you: "Ha!" Gap stores have wonderful sales, as you already know. Anything you want or need should be bought at your local resource.

The outlet stores—which are not really true outlet stores by our definition—sell sale merchandise at the same price it costs on sale in your hometown mall. However, they do have a small amount of style—the best buy is a $10 black mesh tote bag with the words THE GAP FACTORY OUTLET printed outside. Cool, huh?

My girlfriend Mary from Boston says Hingham, Massachusetts, has a decent outlet on Route 3A.

Store locations: Clinton, CT; Freeport, ME; 425 Washington St., downtown Boston

GILLIGAN & O'MALLEY

A sleepwear resource with a Victorian dressy look that provides a more sophisticated look than Lanz, but not as sexy a look as Natori. Good for pretty flannel nightgowns.

Store location: North Conway, NH

GITANO

Jeans for juniors and some other denim fashions and casual clothes. Large stores, big selection. Prices are 25% less than regular retail.

Store locations: Cape Cod, MA; New Bedford, MA; Freeport, ME; Keene, NH

HANES (L'EGGS/HANES/BALI/PLAYTEX)

Makers of cotton-knit underwear for men and women; socks and pantyhose; sweats and active wear—all combined in one store these days. (Also see L'eggs on page 49.)

Store locations: Mystic, CT; Freeport, ME; Kittery, ME; Worcester, MA; North Conway, NH

TOMMY HILFIGER

Upscale Tommy world with fancy outlet stores.

Store locations: Clinton, CT; Worcester, MA

IZOD

No, no, no—it ain't Lacoste any more! Lacoste bought back their name and are now in the midst of a huge comeback. Not only is this not alligator stuff, but I don't know what it is.

Store locations: Clinton, CT; Mystic, CT; Fall River, MA; Kittery, ME; North Conway, NH

 JOAN & DAVID

Outlet stores are very small and consist mostly of a series of shelves or racks organized by size and filled with shoes and some boots. Sizes go up to $10^1/_2$ (women's). Prices range from moderate to high; every now and then you find some styles that are marked to move ($35 to $50). The clothes are so gorgeous I could weep. They are somewhat affordable, but I have to save up or hit a sale.

Store locations: Kittery, ME; Worcester, MA; North Conway, NH

JONES NEW YORK

Moderately priced women's clothing that is almost in the same category as designer bridge clothing. Jones often has a Christian Dior line in stock in the outlets. Great clothes for the career woman on a budget; some weekend wear and some petites.

Store locations: Clinton, CT; New Bedford, MA; Freeport, ME; Manchester, VT

DONNA KARAN

Be still my heart! Wanna hear about the $1,000 three-piece pants outfit I bought for under $500? A mix of DKNY and some of the higher priced items as well as pantyhose (great fit) and accessories.

Store locations: Clinton, CT; Manchester, VT

Anne Klein II

One of the consistently best outlet systems for working women who want good-looking clothes at fairly moderate prices. Most of the stock is Anne Klein II, although a few pieces are from licensed lines and some are from the Anne Klein Collection line. There is always a petites section. You will pay between $200 and $350 for a three-piece suit (all sold as separates), but prices are still less than retail . . . or even retail at their first markdown. Hit a sale at the outlet and you'll never leave. Some accessories are sold; there are runway samples (sizes 6 to 8) sold in a few of the outlet stores.

Store locations: Clinton, CT; Freeport, ME; Kittery, ME; North Conway, NH: Manchester, VT

Calvin Klein

We've never met a Calvin Klein outlet we didn't like, but few of them (outside of New Jersey) carry the expensive line. Most outlet stores are large and architecturally exciting and well stocked with jeans and casual clothes. Some things seem expensive, even at outlet prices; others are more than fairly priced.

Store locations: Clinton, CT; New Bedford, MA; Freeport, ME; Kittery, ME; North Conway, NH; Manchester, VT

Le Creuset

French cast-iron cookware that has been a staple in my home since I was 21 years old (only yesterday). This stuff is known throughout the gourmet cooking world; it weighs a ton and it costs a bundle. I wouldn't dream of buying it full retail. There are only a few outlet stores in the U.S., so drive great distances if need be. They will ship, so you don't have to worry about that Dutch oven in your suitcase.

Store location: Clinton, CT

L'EGGS

L'eggs is a division of Hanes, so the outlet stores sell pantyhose, socks, cotton-knit underwear (for men and women), etc. This is a great resource for stocking up on the basics.

Store locations: Mystic, CT; Freeport, ME; North Conway, NH

LE SPORTSAC

Famous for their nylon luggage and carry-on pieces, tote bags, and travel accessories, these outlets are small but packed with colorful goods at not-so-cheap prices. Look for sale merchandise if you want to find a good deal.

Store locations: Kittery, ME; North Conway, NH

LEVI'S OUTLET

Levi has a very big outlet business; their stores are called Specials, which may be the only sign or name you see on an outlet. The Levi's logo will be in the corner or background. The large stores feature many of the Levi lines, including Dockers, although sometimes you'll find a freestanding Dockers outlet.

Store locations: Bourne, MA; Fall River, MA; Worcester, MA; Kittery, ME; Westbrook, CT

LONDON FOG

They sell a lot more than raincoats! Turn to London Fog for all kinds of outerwear for men and women, some all-weather accessories, and even luggage.

Store locations: Worcester, MA; Fall River, MA; Kittery, ME; North Conway, NH

MAIDENFORM

Prices on this dependable name in underwear and sleepwear are exactly half the regular retail price.

Store locations: Clinton, CT; Plymouth, MA; Worcester, MA

 MALO

This Madison Avenue store that specializes in chic cashmeres now sells cashmere leftovers from this outlet store.

Store location: Clinton, CT

MIKASA

Housewares and tabletop design form this famous maker displayed in outlets that would be at home in any mall in America. Stock up on gifts if you don't need dishes, pitchers, silverware, serving pieces, glassware, or Portuguese-style ceramics.

Store locations: Clinton, CT; Worcester, MA; Freeport, ME; Kittery, ME

NATORI

Without a doubt the fanciest underwear made in America, Natori is expensive at retail and expensive at outlet stores. The stores are usually small with a selection of sleepwear and sets (matching robes or kimonos), but some underwear sets are available.

Store locations: New Bedford, MA; North Conway, NH

NAUTICA

This is a very expensive, prestigious line for the sailing and preppy crowd; there are no real bargains at the outlet store simply because the merchandise is so highly priced to begin with. If you must have Nautica, the outlet does offer 25% or more off regular retail on end-of-the-season goods. New women's line.

Store locations: Clinton, CT; Kittery, ME

NIKE

Now that their retail stores have become theatrical experiences and tourist attractions in major U.S. cities, their outlet stores are mere stores. Just do it. Discontinued styles are 40% off.

Store location: Clinton, CT

 OFF FIFTH

Saks Fifth Avenue has had a few names for their outlet department stores but whatever they call them, I say *yesssss*. Don't get carried away. It is—like all of these places—a hit-or-miss business, but if you get lucky, you can have a good time. There's usually two different seasons worth of merchandise on the floor and the combination of goods that came off the store floor (with SFA tags) and goods that were made for the outlet.

Store locations: Clinton, CT; Worcester, MA

OSHKOSH B'GOSH

Run to OshKosh if you have kids or need gifts for kids. A pair of their famous overalls at $12 is the deal of the century. Europeans consider this a status item, so if you're looking to give a present to friends overseas, consider kids' clothes from OshKosh.

Store locations: Worcester, MA; Kittery, ME; North Conway, NH

 POLO/RALPH LAUREN

I consider Ralph Lauren the king of the outlet business because he had the foresight to see the business for what it could be, to enter with a bang for the buck from the beginning, and to really legitimize outlet shopping. All his outlet stores are similar: large, well stocked, well decorated, and mobbed. Prices range from moderate to low. There are usually some bins selling the famous Polo shirt—marked as damaged—as well as shelves of the perfect, first-quality shirts.

The children's section is pretty good. The housewares selection can be excellent. There are currently 32 outlet stores in the U.S. (three in the Caribbean); each one is a treat.

Store locations: Clinton, CT; Freeport, ME; Kittery, ME; North Conway, NH; Manchester, VT

REEBOK

Reebok sells Reebok, Weebok (the kids' brand), and Rockport in their outlets. Discounts are modest unless they are dumping a not-too-hot style. The green suede walking shoes at $20 a pair were a bargain. But if you have kids, you'll want to know The Pump situation: Yes, they do stock one or two styles of The Pump. Invariably, it will not be the style your child wants. It will be discounted, but not nearly enough to make you care. Sure, you can get a $125 pair of sneakers for $100. If this is your idea of a deal, do let us know. Clothing is also sold.

Store locations: Westbrook, CT; Freeport, ME; North Conway, NH

RIBBON OUTLET

Craft enthusiasts will delight in these stores where ribbon is sold by the full yard. Craft supplies and spools of ribbon; some at discount prices.

Store locations: Mystic, CT; Cape Cod, MA; Plymouth, MA; Freeport, ME; North Hampton, NH

ROCKPORT

Rockport shoes are 40% off here.

Store location: Westbrook, CT

ROYAL DOULTON

Why would anyone go to England? Bone china, Toby mugs, crystal, and even porcelain flowers at prices equal to those in the U.K.

Store locations: Clinton, CT; East Norwalk, CT; New Bedford, MA; Worcester, MA; Kittery, ME

Samsonite

Nice store with a fine stock of various styles, both hard and soft. Some briefcases and carry-ons. Prices are not dirt cheap, but are less than nonsale retail. Watch local luggage-store sale and promotion prices to make sure you're at the advantage here. Excellent quality.

Store location: Kittery, ME

 ## So Fun! Kids

These people need a new name and fast—talk about a turnoff. Unfortunately, they are right—their clothes are so fun. Separates that mix and match with a grown-up color palate; fashionably cool for kids. Prices are not dirt cheap ($27 for a dress; $17 for a jumper) but the things are adorable.

Store location: Clinton, CT

Sperry Top-Sider/Stride Rite

Complete range in styles; spotty availability in sizes. Still, it's great stuff.

Store locations: Worcester, MA; Kittery, ME

 ## Timberland

Growing up in the outlet business with Ralph Lauren for a role model, Timberland delivers a very nice store with a woodsy interior and a lot of gorgeous merchandise. Only about half of it is shoes. This look is considered very statusy both here and in Europe and you will pay dearly for it, even at the outlet.

Store locations: Kittery, ME; North Conway, NH; North Hampton, NH

TOTES

Umbrellas, rain gear, boots, and a number of gimmicky items at good prices make this a worthwhile visit.

Store locations: Cape Cod, MA; Freeport, ME

 ## ELLEN TRACY

Thank God for Ellen Tracy. Along with Anne Klein, she is one of the few reliable sources for fabulous clothes for the woman who wants to look like a million bucks while spending only a few hundred. A suit (three pieces) will end up in the $200-to-$350 range. Many of the color choices are unfamiliar—either this merchandise was made for the outlet business or was cut exclusively for one specific department store. Pay no mind, the styles are current. Petite styles too.

Store locations: North Conway, NH; Manchester, VT

VAN HEUSEN

Great source for bathing suits, tennis clothes, active wear, and summer needs, as well as jackets, outerwear, and casual clothes for fall—mostly for men, but there are some women's things too.

Store location: Clinton, CT; Worcester, MA; North Hampton, NH

VANITY FAIR

Vanity Fair is a huge company with a lot of merchandise lines, so their outlet stores are usually divided accordingly—get bathing suits, underwear, kids' clothing, knits, active wear—everything. Prices are about 50% off. .

Store location: North Dartmouth, MA

VILLEROY & BOCH

This German line must have factories in the U.S. because their outlet stores are so well stocked. You can get pieces from most of their patterns, including the famous Naif pattern. Crystal and glassware are also sold, as well as little tabletop gift items. But bear in mind this warning from our friend Gail who says she has found Villeroy & Boch merchandise to be less expensive at Marshall's than at the outlet stores; she has also found prices vary from one outlet store to the next. You read it here first.

Store location: Kittery, ME

ADRIENNE VITTADINI

Most of the outlet stores are large with a wide selection of clothes from the various Vittadini lines. Shoes and accessories may be available. As much as we adore these clothes, we confess that we find prices better at Loehmann's. Merchandise in the outlets is priced at less than retail, but not at true bargain prices. Always worth a look, of course.

Store locations: New Bedford, MA; Kittery, ME

WARNACO

Usually a supermarket of goods organized by the names of the various lines. The designer underwear can be fabulous, but otherwise you're looking at White Stag ski jackets at good prices and moderately priced clothing for the masses at low enough prices. They do make the Chaps line for Ralph Lauren.

Store locations: Bridgeport, CT; Kittery, ME

WATERFORD/WEDGWOOD

Same price as in England. Full selection on Waterford crystal and gifts; so-so selection on Wedgwood dishes. They ship.

Store location: Kittery, ME

Westpoint Stevens

OK, my girlfriend CB moved to Atlanta and she discovered the Westpoint Stevens clearance center (Ralph Lauren sheets, $3.99) and I called them and they explained to me that they have about 30 outlets dotted around the U.S. with traditional outlet pricing (25% off) and only one clearance center, right there outside Atlanta near where CB lives, and that's where the incredible bargains are. Still, they do make Ralph Lauren sheets and things for their normal outlets, too.

Store location: Clinton, CT

OUT-OF-THE-WAY OUTLETS

. . . .

Following are a few listings for outlets that deserve to be recognized, but may be slightly off the beaten track or in small developments.

Connecticut

Bridgeport   This is home to the Warnaco factory where there are buys on Warnaco goods from firms like White Stag, Chaps by Ralph Lauren, Puritan, etc. The underwear can be especially fancy, as various big-name designers (Valentino, Ungaro) have at one time or another been a Warnaco licensee. Men's, women's, and children's ski clothing is available; this is an excellent source for ski and winter jackets. It is in a rather depressing neighborhood—not for sightseers or the faint of heart. Open daily; Sunday hours 11am to 5pm. Exit 27 off I-95 to Lafayette Street. Turn right at third stoplight, then right on Gregory Street, and head for the parking lot. Call 203/570-8164.

East Norwalk   Take the Metro North train from Grand Central Station in New York to the East Norwalk stop, which is right in the parking lot for this small outlet center. The center is in a real factory and has a few special tenants and some constantly changing shops. It's certainly worth the trip just to shop **The Company Store,** which sells many upscale ready-to-wear lines for men and women and has Dooney & Bourke leather goods at very good prices. There's about a dozen outlets, including **Royal Doulton** and **Harve Benard.** Take Exit 16 off I-95 and head for East Avenue. The outlets have a huge water tower with their names on it. The building is peach and orange; you can't miss it. Call 203/226-8731.

Norwalk Center Right downtown in Norwalk Center, there are a few freestanding outlet stores that should thrill and delight. **Decker's** (692 West Ave.) has discounted high-end merchandise for everyone in the family. About half this store sells men's clothing; the other half is divided between women's and children's. There isn't a full range and anything goes—we've seen sweaters from Paul Stuart, boy's Polo shirts, women's Ralph Lauren, John Smedley from London, and Giorgio Armani. Cashmere sweaters are always sold for less than London prices.

Half a block away is **Boston Traders Kids** outlet, then head back toward I-95 on West Avenue, you'll end up at **Loehmann's** right before the highway. Also at Loehmann's Plaza you'll find the new, fancy-schmancy **Villeroy & Boch** outlet store with all the popular patterns, some glassware, and many gift ideas. You can find a fabulous wedding gift in the $25 range. If you prefer contemporary style, there's a large **Dansk** outlet store around the corner on Route 1. Before you get to Dansk, you may want to pop in at the **C. R. Gibson** factory store (39 Knight St.), across from the factory itself, where paper goods and cards are 25% less than regular retail. These designer paper plates and other wax-coated paper goods turn any party into a real celebration. You can also buy picture frames, scrapbooks, note cards, gift wrap, and cards at a fraction of their retail price. There's always a summer sale; the winter sale can be in December or January. To get on the mailing list for the dates of the big sale events, call 203/ 847-4543.

Massachusetts

Fall River   Although this city has a big reputation as an outlet center and has several different malls packed with outlet stores, there is very little for the high-end shopper in Fall River. There is fun to be had, and some big names, but when you are combining Fall River, New Bedford, and North Dartmouth in the same day, you may have to make choices. And you may find that Fall River does not offer the expensive merchandise you crave at discount. The outlets are in rehabbed factories in a part of town called The Outlet District. All are close together, although not within walking distance. We loved **Tower Outlet Center** (Converse, Toy Liquidators, Izod, and several jobbers selling names that cannot be advertised); we thought **Quality Factory Outlets** was the next best of show (Bass, Ribbon Outlet, Corning/Revere); we had a good time exploring the freestanding **Louis Hand Curtain Factory** (847 Pleasant St.), located in a real factory. There were a number of good buys in curtains, fabrics, and trims, most in traditional or colonial styles.

New Bedford   The home of **Howland Place,** a factory-outlet mall that started out great guns and is still adding tenants. This is a small mall that tries to have more upscale clients than others. Many are designers with no other outlet store or other New England venue, like Alexon, First Choice, and Putumayo. Tenants include: Calvin Klein, Natori, Adrienne Vittadini, Carmelo Pomodoro, Alexander Julian, Putumayo, Royal Doulton, Gitano, First Choice, He-Ro Group, Alexon, and Vakko Leather. An antiques and artisans gallery is on the fourth level of the restored mill.

North Dartmouth   As you are driving along I-95 from Fall River to New Bedford, you may (or may not) catch a billboard for the **VF Outlet Mall.** There's a huge Vanity Fair, natch, as well as American Tourister, Cape Isle Knitters, and a few others. (If you are headed toward New Bedford, get off at Exit 13, Faunce Corner Road, and turn left.) The outlet center is sort of in the middle of nowhere.

Lenox   So, you're driving through the Berkshires, and you aren't interested in Jacob's Pillow and Norman Rockwell, and all you really want is a little discount shopping. Well, step this way: This small mall called **Lenox House Country Shops & Outlets** includes Adolfo, Bass Shoe, Corning/Revere, Harve Benard, L'eggs, The Ribbon Outlet, and Quoddy Shoes. Take Exit 2 from I-90 or stay on Route 7 until you bump into the outlet at the junction of 7 and 7A.

Lawrence   This small mall is not much but it's close to New Hampshire, and it does have yippy skippy, Polo/Ralph Lauren. There's also Bugle Boy and several big-name sport-shoe outlet stores. It's called **Everett Mills;** take Exit 45 from I-495.

New Hampshire

Keene   This midsize mall has enough big names to make it worth the stop if you are in the neighborhood. It's close to both Vermont and Massachusetts. Tenants include: Aileen, Bass Shoe, Harve Benard, Gitano, The Ribbon Outlet, Toy Liquidators, and Quoddy Shoes. Heading north on I-91, take Exit 3 and follow signs to Keene. The outlet center is on Ralston Street.

Manchester   This is Manchester, New Hampshire, not Vermont, so don't get too excited. Still there are camps and a university nearby so you might want to hit **Pandora Outlet Center** for Burlington Coat Factory, Carter's Childrenswear, and Kayser Roth, etc. Exit I-293 at Canal and Dow streets.

Vermont

Brattleboro Outlet Center   I thought this looked so boring I didn't even want to stop, especially since we were on our way to Manchester. Warm up here with **Carter's Childrenswear, L'eggs, Van Heusen,** and a few others. Going north on I-91, take Exit 1 to Canal Street.

Chapter Five

. . . .

ANTIQUES & CRAFTS

COLLECTING THE FUTURE

. . . .

I can't decide if crafts have always been collectible or if they've become hot because people with traditional homes like to shop for antiques and people with contemporary homes have nothing to shop for. Regardless, crafts are one of the major statements of this decade, and not just because they're beautiful—that combination of art and culture makes a statement about our times. Any object that is unique, especially a beautiful, handmade one, has value. When made to last, it also has value as a collectible. There are many who regret being born too late to get in on impressionist paintings when they were going for peanuts; they're now buying crafts and hoping to get in on the ground floor of a movement.

So whether you shop for the ground floor, or for granny's attic, you'll find that New England is home to more craftspeople and more antiques dealers than just about any part of America.

ANTIQUE DREAMS: COUNTRY AUCTIONS

. . . .

I've been on the prowl for affordable antiques in New England for many years now and I've realized that antiques shopping breaks down into two distinct categories: People who want high-end collectibles and have their own dealers, sources, budgets, and agendas, and those who are more like us.

I like what serious collectors might term "junk." And we like it cheap—that is to say, inexpensive. I prefer to shop at tag sales and yard sales. I'm fond of auctions (and I don't mean those at Sotheby's).

Of course, New England has its share of fancy auctions, of branches of big-name houses and auction snobs. You can find all that and you may even enjoy it. But I like the kind of auction that's held under a tent on a country road. I like it when prices are so low you want to weep . . . and buy.

Generally, auctions do not follow a regular yearly schedule except to say that big-city and fancy auctions are usually in fall and winter and country auctions are usually in summer. Fancy auctions in resort locations (for example, Nantucket) are also in summer.

Some auctions are held on a prescheduled basis in the summer season as annual events; others are held a few times throughout the year with dates posted and announced as you go. Viewings are usually held a few hours immediately prior to the auction, unless you're talking about a big-time auction house.

The buying of unknown lots, sight unseen, is common. You may find the competition stiff or the market wide open. Where you stand to gain the most is in any area where you have some degree of expertise. Never bid on anything unless you know its real value (unless, of course, you can't live without it).

To get started on some country auctions, contact these auctioneers:

Norman C. Heckler & Co.
Bradford Corner Row
Woodstock Valley, CT 06282
☎ 203/974-1634

Litchfield Auction Co.
P.O. Box 1337, Route 202
Litchfield, CT 06415
☎ 203/567-3126

Nadeau's Auction Gallery
489 Old Hartford Rd.
Colchester, CT 06415
☎ 203/537-3888

F. O. Bailey Antiquarians
141 Middle St.
Portland, ME 04101
☎ 207/774-1479

Barridoff Galleries (Fine Art)
P.O. Box 9715
Portland, ME 04104
☎ 207/772-5011

James D. Julia, Inc.
P.O. Box 830
Fairfield, ME 04937
☎ 207/453-7904

Maritime Auctions
P.O. Box 322
York, ME 03909
☎ 207/363-4247

Richard W. Oliver, Inc.
Plaza One
Kennebunk, ME 04043
☎ 207/985-3600

Robert O. Stuart Auction Co.
P.O. Box 104
Limington, ME 04049
☎ 207/793-4522

James R. Baker
370 Broadway
Cambridge, MA 02139
☎ 617/864-7067

Richard A. Bourne Co., Inc.
P.O. Box 141
Hyannisport, MA 02647
☎ 508/775-0797

Bradford Galleries, Ltd.
Route 7, Box 160
Sheffield, MA 02157
☎ 413/229-6667

Fontaine's Auction Gallery
173 S. Mountain Rd.
Pittsfield, MA 01201
☎ 413/448-8922

Grogan & Co. (Fine Art)
890 Commonwealth Ave.
Boston, MA 02215
☎ 617/566-4100

Willis Henry Auctions, Inc.
22 Main St.
Marshfield, MA 02050
☎ 617/834-7774

Rafael Osona
P.O. Box 2607
Nantucket, MA 02584
☎ 508/228-3942

Skinner, Inc.
357 Main St.
Bolton, MA 01740
☎ 508/779-6241

Paul McInnis
Route 88
Hampton Falls, NH 03844
☎ 603/778-8989

Ronald J. Rosenbleeth, Inc.
28 Western Ave.
Henniker, NH 03242
☎ 603/428-7686

Richard W. Withington, Inc.
590 Center Rd.
Hillsboro, NH 03244
☎ 603/464-3232

Road Runner Auctions
7 Quaker Lane
W. Warwick, RI 02893
☎ 401/826-1441

Duane Merrill
James Brown Drive
Williamstown, VT 05679
☎ 802/878-2625

Sir Richard's Enterprises
Route 100
Waterbury Center, VT 05677
☎ 802/244-8879

NEW ENGLAND YARD SALES

. . . .

Someday I will write the book on tag sales. It will include all our triumphs: The Clarice Cliff dishes we bought for $40; the 10 place settings of Wedgwood for $300; the armchair for $25; the genuine Chanel earrings for $10 a pair, and more.

Yard sales, which are also called tag sales, are a way of life you may quickly become addicted to if you're a serious shopper in search of a bargain.

Indeed, some of what we have bought while enjoying our excursions into other peoples' homes and garages has had true value (those Clarice Cliff dishes are worth a bundle); much of it was worth more than we paid for it. All of it was fun to buy and was a bargain in our eyes—whether it has real value or not.

Once you get hooked on tag sales, you'll find your decorating style turns on your ability and willingness to make do with what's available and to recognize potential in its raw form. For example: I pictured the powder room with a pair of floral wrought-iron country-French candle sconces, one on each side of the mirror. I saw exactly the pair we wanted at Pierre Deux for $165. A bit rich . . . so when I found an unattractive pair of dark wooden sconces at a tag sale for $4, we were happy to buy them, strip them, and antique-finish them. True, they're wood, not metal, and more colonial than Provençal. But you know what? For $4, I love them!

When the price is right, you're hindered only by the limits of your imagination. Tag sales are for those with vision and patience. You'll see a lot of junk as you comb tag sales; you will "waste" a lot of time. You will hardly ever find what you need when you need it. But if you love the thrill of the chase and hate all other prices (even discounted retail), you'll lose your heart to a new way of life. To find tag sales, read local papers or follow the handwritten signs that dot country back roads on weekends.

CONSIGNMENT SHOPS

When New Englanders want to clean house to get rid of what they think of as junk, they have a yard sale. When they think the same junk has some value, they take it to a consignment shop. The person who supplies the stock gets a percentage of the sale price; the owner of the consignment shop provides the roof, the sales help, and the expertise to price and market the items.

While consignment shops are all over New England, we usually find them overpriced. Granted, I've been ruined by tag-sale prices, but still . . . not only do I find prices high, but the owners often seem unwilling to negotiate.

Although there are some consignment shops that feature clothes (usually "gently worn" designer pieces), the best shops sell furniture and decorative arts. In fact, you might wander into one and assume it is an antiques shop. The state of Connecticut seems to have a plethora of antiques shops like this while Newbury Street in Boston is heavy on resale shops for clothing.

ATTENTION INTERNATIONAL SHOPPERS

English and European visitors who appreciate quality should branch out to tag sales and consignment shops for even greater triumphs. Among the recent successes Ian took back to England: Brooks Brothers navy-blue down-filled ski jacket ($10); leather-and-canvas suitcase ($3); Harris tweed Daniel Hechter sports jacket ($6); wide wale cords ($3 per pair); paperback best-sellers (50¢ each). Prices are just unbelievable.

BOOKING ANTIQUES

Antiques and Art Directory: This annual travel guide is available in antiques shops around New England, if not in bookstores. The book consists of listings and ads from antiques shops all over New England and New York's Hudson River Valley. There's a show calendar in the back.

Sloan's Guide to Antiquing in New England: A larger-sized format than the *Antiques and Art Directory,* and more evenly distributed in regular bookstores, this guide is still very similar to the competition, although there aren't any big ads or color pictures.

Antiques and the Arts Weekly: This is the one we subscribe to, so naturally we think it's the best . . . the newspaper format has editorials about collectibles, lots of ads, announcements of fairs, markets, antiques shows, auctions, and reports on what's been sold or changed hands. Despite the fancy title, most people in the trade call this *The Bee.* Published by The Bee Publishing, 5 Church Hill Rd., Newtown, CT 06470 (☎ 203/426-3141).

The Magazine Antiques: This very serious monthly is glossy, gorgeous, and educational. There is some New England advertising with pictures so you can get a feel for the high-end dealers; there's always a pullout regional section with a map.

The Antiques Directory & Traveler's Guide: A seasonal travel guide available at newsstands and antiques shops with listings, show calendar, and a fair amount of advertising. Has changed publishers and title slightly while the book itself has remained constant. Published by August Enterprises, Inc., 63 Hillside Ave., Melrose, MA 02176.

New England Antiques Journal: Newspaper-style like *The Bee* with some color pictures. Write to: 4 Church St., Ware, MA 01082.

Mass Bay Antiques: This monthly is handed out free in many Boston and Boston area antiques shops and shows—you can also buy a subscription to this newspaper-style publication. Published by North Shore Weeklies, P.O. Box 293, 9 Page St., Danvers, MA 01923.

The Boston Globe: The Sunday edition has an auctions section as well as listings of shows and some yard sales. The Thursday Calendar section of the *Globe* features weekend entertainment ideas as well as local fairs and antiques events.

STORE HOURS

. . . .

One of the reasons people go into the antiques business is that it gives them flexibility in hours, in place of business, in ability to go to shows and travel. It's not unusual for hours to be posted simply as BY CHANCE. Many dealers, especially the successful ones, operate by appointment only. Late mornings are the rule. Weekends may be devoted to shows.

SHOWS

. . . .

Antiques shows and fairs are the backbone of the business as well as part of the lure of New England. Will you find bargains? Maybe, maybe not. Much depends on what you are looking for, quality, etc. We've found that smaller shows with 50 or fewer dealers and a high admission ($5 a head) don't give us our money's worth. We prefer bigger shows (300 to 600 dealers) and no admission, but will pay for a good show with lots of dealers. Hoity-toity shows do not impress us.

You may want to pay additional admission charges (usually $25 per head) for early admission to a big show—dealers find this worthwhile as do serious collectors. Sometimes early admission is related to a charitable event.

Shows are most often sponsored by professionals who become known for a certain style of show (and for attracting a certain style of exhibitor); you can write them for a complete calendar or find their ads in antiques trade publications and the *Antiques Directory*. Freebie announcements to future shows are always handed out at events.

Outdoor shows tend to be in spring and summer, while indoor events are held in the winter. The New England season is more geared to summer; England and Europe provide more serious action in the winter.

BIG SUMMER SHOWS

· ·

Brimfield, MA: Three shows a year: May, July, and early September. See page 72 for more.

Great Barrington, MA: Two different Berkshire fairs are held at the fairgrounds here, so that both June and July offer something special. Also Ephemera markets. Call 508/744-2731 for dates.

Farmington, CT: Three times a year this good-sized fair (600 vendors) dazzles those who want something less stressful than Brimfield. Early buying allowed; call 508/839-9735 for dates. The summer show is usually the first week in June; there is also a September show. You can take a chartered bus from New York; for bus information call 800/344-7469.

Woodstock, VT: This central Vermont community has a good reputation for its interest in antiques; toward the end of July they usually have a well-attended event. Call 802/435-2034 to get the show office for dates.

Maine Antiques Festival: Weekend event usually held in August at the fairgrounds in Union—over 300 dealers. This is an indoor-outdoor event; early buying is allowed. Call 207/563-1013.

New Haven, CT: Annual antiques show that has been going on for over 50 years. Call 203/387-7006 for dates and information.

ANTIQUES CENTERS

· ·

ANTIQUE CENTER OF NORTHAMPTON
9¹/₂ Market St., Northampton, MA

A multidealer deal; about an hour from Brimfield in the crafty town of Northampton (see page 91). Slightly off the main shopping street but still within walking distance; there are three levels of shops here.

HADLEY ANTIQUES CENTER
Rte. 9, Hadley, MA

Some 70 dealers in this community in the Pioneer Valley, not far from Northampton. There is also a Sunday flea market in Hadley beginning in late April, as weather permits. The flea market is at Exit 19 off I-91 North. Closed Wednesday.

KENNEDY BROTHERS
Rte. 22A, Vergennes, VT

No, not those Kennedy brothers. This is a mill that's been turned into a shopping area and antiques center with about 150 dealers. Great fun. Also crafts and other stuff in this rehab.

KNOTTY PINE ANTIQUE MARKET
Rte. 10, West Swanzey, NH

Some 300 dealers; admission is $2 per head or a business card if you are in the trade. This is right near Keene. Open daily.

NEW BEDFORD ANTIQUES COMPANY
85 Coggeshall St., New Bedford, MA

Large space in a former warehouse with about 250 dealers. Right on the edge of the highway, so it's convenient.

OLDE BYFIELD EXPO CENTRE
12 Kent Way, Byfield, MA

Very touristy mart; new center for 300 dealers plus show and auction space. A little more than a half hour north of Boston. Daily 10am to 5pm; take Exit 55 off of I-95.

TIMBER VILLAGE ANTIQUE CENTER
Rte. 4, White River, VT

Some 300 dealers exhibit at this popular center, which is said to be the largest in Vermont. Near Woodstock.

WELLS ANTIQUE MART
Rte. 1, Wells, MA

Sort of an indoor flea market with just under 100 dealers; a source frequented by the trade.

THE ANTIQUES SCENE: BOSTON

The two best antiques neighborhoods in the city of Boston are: Newbury Street, which is not as hoity-toity as it sounds—you'll find both big-time dealers and mom-and-pop shops where they sell Fiestaware dishes and a few vintage record albums; and Beacon Hill, where your stroll down Charles Street will give you the benefit of a number of high- and medium-end shops. See page 152 for Newbury Street details; see page 155 for more on Beacon Hill.

After you've done the big city, get your *Boston Globe* and check on neighborhood yard sales or head to some of the suburbs for antiques shops and centers. You'll find a host of them dotting the north and south shore area. Essex, 30 minutes north of Boston (closer than Salem!), has almost 25 antiques dealers, most located on Main Street (Route 133). In the other direction is New Bedford, which has a great antiques center (see above).

THE ANTIQUES SCENE: BRIMFIELD, MA

Brimfield is not very far from Sturbridge. Everyone's heard of Sturbridge, but only antiques junkies know about Brimfield. In fact, it's not the town of Brimfield they know about, but the three-times-a-year antiques market that is held there. These are 10-day fairs made up of a week and the weekends on either end.

In reality, Brimfield consists of dozens of markets, making for a gigantic shopping spree at which over 3,000 dealers of country arts (very little new merchandise is sold) will set up under tents or in open fields and negotiate. This used to be open to the trade only, but has caught on with the public over the past few years to become quite an event. During the fairs, official markets spring up in various places and unofficial tag sales dot the landscape all the way from Sturbridge. We begin to pant. We grow faint. We book a hotel a year in advance. We are serious about Brimfield.

Shows are held the first week in May and July, and after the first week of September. Different shows are on different days of the week. The first 2 days of the show are the best. Rumor has it that the May and September shows are better than the July show. Events are rain or shine; be prepared. Jeans and jackets are OK—this is not Paris. The market has a very different feel depending on which fields are open. My favorites are J & J and May's (see below); I schedule myself for those days.

Some markets open at daybreak, others at 6am. We've heard crazy stories of people standing in line at dawn, then breaking down the fences to run around with fists full of dollars. We went at 6am once only to discover no one was moving. There was still plenty to see, to do, and to buy at 8am and at 10am. Dealers start to knock off for the day between 5pm and 6pm.

The best thing to do is park as close to the center of town—and the action—as you can and then walk to the fair. Parking may cost $3. Some people work with a wagon or a grocery pull cart so they can load up before taking their haul to the car. We bring the station wagon, but if you're a serious shopper you may want to come with a U-Haul. A few of the markets charge admission; most don't. The ones that do charge are the good ones, so save up. Sometimes the parking fee is included in the admission charge.

J & J Promoters

I think this is the best field and we always start here. Furthermore, we've even learned not to come to Brimfield on a day when they are not open. About 700 dealers. May be open only 2 days of the fair. Admission charged. Located on Route 20. Call 413/245-3436 for their specific show dates.

May's Antique Market

Almost across the street from J & J and a little more funky, but it's our next stop. About 600 dealers. Open for only 3 days. Admission charged. Located on Route 20; ☎ 413/245-9271.

THE ANTIQUES SCENE: NEWPORT, RI

Yes, yes, of course some of the people who live in Newport are antiques. And the houses and house tours and hoopla surrounding your peek into a way of life wiped out by World War I and income tax can be an education in art and antiques as well. Beyond that, there are a number of shops to pop into to complete your retail experience in Newport.

Franklin and Spring streets are the ones to head to for a variety of antiques ranging from formal to funky. Walk and browse; make sure to check out the following shops:

On Franklin Street: **All Things Oriental** (no. 8); **What Not Shop** (no. 16); **Jill Oltz** (no. 24); **Anchor & Dolphin Books** (no. 30); **J. B. Antiques** (no. 33); **Ransom House Antiques** (no. 34); **Teresa Cook** (no. 38½); **A & A Gaines Fine Antiques** (no. 40); **Smith Marble Antiques** (no. 44).

On Spring Street: **Simmons & Simmons** (no. 223); **Antiques Drawing Room** (no. 221); **Antiques at Ethel's Old Place** (no. 223); **Richard's** (no. 42); **New England Antiques** (no. 60).

THE ANTIQUES SCENE: NEW PRESTON, CT

New Preston has a magical reputation as an insider's source for antiques. Magazines continue to write such glowing reports that you feel your life will never be complete until you, too, have made the pilgrimage. So we have a very controversial report for you: New Preston is a glorious and terrible place to shop.

Yes, it is that confusing. First of all, New Preston is not much of a city. We were expecting a main street, a place to park and stroll, some New England charm—after all, magazine articles had been written about this place. Instead, New Preston is merely a bend in the road at the junction of Route 202N and Route 45—a flash of adorable stores you'll miss if you blink.

Most of these stores do indeed sell antiques and do so in a splendid environment. Never have we seen so many stores with a design point of view; so much patina in a retail sense. And never have we seen such highfalutin' prices, such a clever mix of old and new and repro posing as antique—such nerve, such chutzpah, such hubris.

There is no question that these stores are charming and that we, too, would like to open our own shop right here by the creek and the rehabs. Maybe we'll call it "Presumption." Until we get the place going, the town has its own attractions; almost every store is a find.

Hours vary. Some stores are open only Thursday through Monday. Most are open from 11am to 5pm. A few open earlier. Sunday hours are from noon to 5pm.

Finds

BLACK SWAN ANTIQUES
Rte. 45, New Preston, CT

More formal than any of the other dealers, with an air of serious English quality, although there is some furniture that is country in design and feel and some American antiques that are somewhat Federal.

NEW PRESTON ANTIQUES CENTER
Church St., New Preston, CT

Most of the antiques centers we've been in offer merchandise from different dealers, different time periods, and different thoughts on the merits of style. This shop is at peace with itself and of one piece in terms of what it's selling—a very sophisticated country look with a touch of whimsy. Located behind the Main Street store.

JONATHAN PETERS
5 Main St., New Preston, CT

This is our favorite shop in town; we're ready to move in. The space is sort of ethereal with lots of white-work linens and dried flowers. Dishes and many new craft items are stacked around. Everything is light and dreamy and not too cheap. We wanted to take home an old basket filled with dried white roses: $265. Oh well.

J. SEITZ & CO.
9 E. Shore Dr., New Preston, CT

For those of you concerned with the sociological history of the place, word has it that Jane Seitz had a wonderful store in New Milford and then moved to New Preston, bringing her wit, charm, and style with her—and the rest of the stores bloomed in order to catch up. Bloom on, Jane. Although we grow weary of Santa Fe style (especially outside of New Mexico), this store combines Southwestern chic with cowboy-and-Indian looks, Mexican arts and crafts, and a few other touches to make it work . . . and work for New England. There's mostly clothing, but you can also find hand-painted furniture, blankets (old Beacon and new Pendleton), crafts, cookery, accessories, Mexican glass, and all kinds of surprises. This is the only store in the group that doesn't specialize in antiques. So why is it in our antiques section? Well, the hand-painted furniture goes with the antiques and country looks. So there.

THE TRUMPETEER
5 Main St., New Preston, CT

Next door to Jonathan Peters, this store looks like it's straight out of the pages of a magazine (although most of the stores in New Preston have that same quality) and sells a combination of old prints, autographs, costume pieces, and small items that look or feel antique, but may not be. Absolutely charming and delightful. Magnifying glasses like the ones we bought in London for $50 cost $125 here.

THE ANTIQUES SCENE: WOODBURY, CT

I was reading an article in a fancy magazine, maybe *Architectural Digest*, about someone who was asked to take Jacqueline Kennedy Onassis antiquing and so she took her to Woodbury. I like Woodbury, regardless of Mrs. Onassis, because its about a half hour from New Preston, so together they make a satisfying day. On their own, I find each lacking.

Emotionally, Woodbury is a totally different kind of place from New Preston. You can't just park your car and walk everywhere—things are spread out and you must continually move your car.

There are about 30 dealers spread across Main Street with addresses written either as Main Street North or Main Street South. Hours are pretty much standard around town: 11am to 5pm Tuesday through Saturday, and Sundays 1 to 5pm. Some stores open earlier on Saturdays; not all stores are closed on Mondays. But Mondays aren't a good idea because so many stores are shuttered.

---

free Directory

For a directory of the shops (with map), write the
Woodbury Antiques Dealers Association, P.O. Box
496, Woodbury, CT 06798.

COUNTRY LOFT
88 Main St. N., Woodbury, CT

Country Loft is not only the picture-perfect barn
stocked with stock—everything you want it to be—
but it is one of the few Souleiado dealers in the U.S.,
meaning they have the goods that used to be sold in
Pierre Deux shops (but no longer are).

The look is country, not just Provençal, so the
French country touches work but this is not just for
French country fanatics; it's for anyone who enjoys
the ooohs and aaaaahs of discovered delights.

BRITISH COUNTRY ANTIQUES
50 Main St., Woodbury, CT

Far more plain and simple with pine and clean lines;
there's a house and a barn full of stuff. Closed on
Monday and Tuesday.

MILL HOUSE ANTIQUES
1068 Main St. N., Woodbury, CT

This is like a museum of shops; there are showrooms
sprawled across the estate on 200 acres. Although
the store is closed on Tuesday like everyone else,
they have extra Sunday hours so the weekend shoppers can get a good go at it. The store opens at
9:30am Saturday and Sunday.

WAYNE PRATT
345 Main St. S., Woodbury, CT

You know him in Nantucket. Formal country and formal European. No junk. High prices. Yummy. Also closed Monday and Tuesday.

THE ANTIQUES SCENE: SHEFFIELD, MA

Cute? You want cute? You want fantasy? Do you want to drive into a town and see a ton of antiques shops all beckoning you to stop? Welcome to Sheffield, a great place to poke around and stay a day . . . or two. Maybe you should move here. Sheffield has been going strong since before the Revolutionary War and still appears as an early-American town . . . with a lot of freestanding antiques shops situated in many of the Main Street (Route 7) homes. Although the houses are a bit too spread out to walk from one to another, you can simply drive along the main street and stop at any of the nearly 60 shops that line the 2-mile stretch. By the time you reach Sheffield Pottery, the shopping peters out.

If you're really into this, before you get to Sheffield, right before you cross into Massachusetts, veer off to the left (if you're heading north) and take Route 7A on the slow road to nowhere. At Ashley Falls, there are several yummy antiques dealers to whet your appetite for Sheffield. Then take 7A right back to Route 7 just south of Sheffield and shop some more.

All of the following stores are on Route 7. Keep your eyes peeled.

Bradford Galleries, Ltd.: Once a month there's an auction, tourists or not. Big secret for locals and dealers. They also have an appraisal business. Call 413/229-6667 for a printed summer or fall schedule.

Cupboards and Roses: This store sells quasi-antiques, but does offer the country look New England is famous for. Since we've been nuts for painted furniture for a few years now, we suggest you take a

Free Directory

To be totally prepared for your antiques spree, you might want to write ahead and get a free booklet listing all 60 area dealers. Write to: Berkshire County Massachusetts Antiques Dealers Association, RR #1, Box 1-AAG, Sheffield, MA 02157; ☎ 413/229-2628.

look at the stuff here, which includes locally made and European goods.

Darr Antiques: This is your fantasy store. The house is a living antiques shop furnished with 18th- and 19th-century European and American treasures. Also a few Asian pieces. A tad formal, very fine; two separate buildings.

Down the Rabbit Hole: OK, so it's not an antiques store. You'll just have to humor us so we can slip this in. This is one of the best-known crafts galleries in the area and prides itself on representing the best New England artists. If you aren't going to Northampton, Massachusetts, this may be an opportunity to see, learn, and acquire contemporary crafts works. Just south of town.

Kuttner Antiques: Formal furniture from England—and some American, too—also decorative arts and porcelain. As is the trend in Sheffield, 18th and 19th century is the specialty.

Susan Silver: Good reputation through New England for the selection of formal English and country-French furniture from the 18th and 19th centuries.

THE ANTIQUES SCENE: STAMFORD, CT

Stamford does not really have an antiques scene. It is the home of **United House Wrecking** (535 Hope St.), a resource that has grown to mythical proportions. Twenty years ago you could get great bathtubs, fireplaces, and doors at low prices: hence the reputation. Now the place is a TT (Tourist Trap) for antiques and imports. Prices are not particularly low. The space is large, mostly indoors, and stuff is crammed everywhere. The problem is that fewer homes seem to be demolished and more tag-sale finds seem to be displayed—at large markups. It's fun if you are in the neighborhood, but don't make a special trip. Open daily.

CRAFTILY YOURS

Trend forecasters predict the big collectibles of the future—in terms of getting a leg up on investment—are crafts. New England makes it easy for you to start or continue your trendsetting pace.

Crafts are an important part of the New England landscape. Every main street of every shopping city has at least one crafts gallery. People in New England don't want to be part of the Paris or New York fashion scene. They are the kind of people who wear simple clothes, read good books, and believe in the importance of the one-of-a-kind workmanship that is at the heart of the crafts movement. Many states brag about how many craftspeople are in residence (New Hampshire for instance); other cities stake their reputation in the marketplace based on the abundance of the works available (like Northampton, Massachusetts). Crafts fairs pop up everywhere, especially in the summer; juried and vetted fairs are known and followed by devotees.

BOOKING CRAFTS

If you're serious about collecting, it pays to do some research up front. There are several magazines devoted to crafts in general and to specific art forms. A few suggestions to get you started:

American Craft: Published bimonthly; $45 a year. Contact ACC, 45 W. 45th St., New York, NY 10036.

American Ceramics: Published quarterly; $28 a year. Contact the magazine at 9 E. 45th Street, New York, NY 10017.

Fiberarts: Published five times a year; $20 a year. Write Nine Press, 50 College St., Asheville, NC 28805.

Warning: The reason there are juried and vetted crafts shows (with expert judges) is that everyone in America thinks his or her own crafts projects are good enough to sell. There are tons of little fairs and garage sales and events where crafts are sold, and the work is—how can I put this delicately—well, *amateur.* When you go to a juried show, there is usually an admission charge, but you get the really good stuff and have more assurance that you aren't wasting your time and money.

BUYING CRAFTS

· ·

Some people buy what talks to them; some buy a piece from a certain artist whenever they can afford to do so; some collect in specific categories. For the most part, buying crafts is a matter of the heart and soul meeting the pocketbook. Many times you will have the opportunity to talk with the artist, to get a better feel for his or her work. Price should reflect intricacy, expertise, and reputation.

Crafts are traditionally bought from galleries, which act much as department stores: They keep 40% or 50% of the retail price. With depression and recession in the air, more shoppers and more craftspeople are willing to go the distance to sell outside of the galleries. This means the artist will sell a piece for less than the gallery price and the shopper will seek out the artist at his or her studio. It can be fun . . . or awkward.

Most craftspeople work out of their homes or in nearby studios; most work spaces are not open to the public on a regular basis. However, a large number of artists will make an appointment to see you if they are in residence and able to take a break. Usually they are more available on weekdays, as many artists go to fairs on weekends. It's not considered polite to simply drop in; you can call from a pay phone and say, "I'm in the neighborhood and I've heard about your work. I wonder if I could stop by?" Don't bring the family, the kids, the dog, and the diaper bag. Be sure to ask the artist if there is a minimum order *before* you stop by. No use wasting time and energy—on either side. A large percentage of the big-name craftspeople have a $300 minimum order for shows; they may or may not waive this for home visits. Ask.

For a directory of the major players, with their addresses and phone numbers, get a copy of the ACC (American Craft Council) Annual Directory (see below), which lists every artist who shows with them. This is a national round-up; only a percentage of the artists are from New England.

FAIR THEE WELL

. . . .

The largest New England fair is the annual ACC Craft Fair, which is held in West Springfield, Massachusetts (at the fairgrounds), in the early summer. There is a winter ACC Fair also, but it's held in Baltimore. Both of these markets attract almost 1,000 artists. They are big-time events with both trade days and days when the event is open to the paying public.

Many state tourist offices will provide free information on craftspeople and fairs and events, usually in the form of an annual (or seasonal) guide. State and local crafts associations also can provide information, as can the American Craft Council. Don't forget that New England's many Shaker communities are very involved in crafts. To get you started, make a few calls and start to network:

American Craft Council: ☎ 800/836-3470; ☎ 914/883-6100; fax 914/883-6130

League of New Hampshire Craftsmen: ☎ 603/224-1471

Vermont State Craft Fair: ☎ 802/674-6720

Frog Hollow Crafts Center (Vermont): ☎ 802/388-3177

Berkshire Crafts Fair (Massachusetts): ☎ 413/528-3346 or ☎ 607/265-3230

Maine Crafts Association: ☎ 207/348-9943

DIRECTORY OF FAVORITE CRAFTSPEOPLE

· ·

Sweaters, Weavers, Yarns

ROBIN L. BERGMAN
Lexington, MA; ☎ *617/862-1121*

If you have ever craved a sweater, jacket, or coat that merged art, color, Koos Van Der Akker, and the Missonis with original style, taste, and whimsy, then you must see the work of Robin Bergman, who creates one-of-a-kind hand-loomed clothes. Prices are in the $300-to-$600 range—and deservedly so. The coat we'd die for costs $1,200.

FRANCES FRANCIS
Eastham, MA; ☎ *508/255-3390*

Coats, jackets, shawls, and more from home-woven fiber. Some of the weavings are worked with brocade, which makes for a rich and unusual combination of texture and style.

CYNTHIA KRAUSE
Leverett, MA; ☎ *413/584-9925*

Almost medieval-style tunics, vests, stoles, and things so unique and classical only Robin Hood will be your match. Prices range from $100 to $150, although scarves at $30 make a wonderful gift.

PENFRYDD WOOLS
Colrain, MA; ☎ *413/624-5516*

For every knitter (or craftsperson) who has dreamed of color and texture, this is the resource that will make you quit the real world and sit home and knit. If you do not know how to knit, one look at these hand-dyed wools will set you to learning.

Fiber Arts

HERZENBERG
Holyoke, MA; ☎ *413/584-5099*

Hand-painted silk neckties. Some in traditional styles, others wild and wonderful. Best hand-painted ties we've seen in ages.

CACOPHONY
Cambridge, MA; ☎ *617/491-4025*

Knitted quilts that are works of art and heirlooms in the making. Buy a baby-sized one as a gift, pillows for an artistic statement, or a big one-of-a-kind masterpiece if you are investing in the future.

Baskets

MATTHEW S. NEWMAN
New Braintree, MA; ☎ *617/867-3318*

Matt makes a basket that is at once traditional in form and contemporary in statement. We think he's one of the most outstanding artists crafting baskets today. He harvests and creates from local woods; his baskets do have a design patent.

SYLVIA SIMPSON
Montpelier, VT; ☎ *802/229-0953*

Vibrantly colored baskets made from telephone wire and non–ecologically correct findings that are bright, hot, creative, and contemporary. Moderate prices make these baskets even more attractive.

STEPHEN ZEH
Temple, ME; ☎ *207/778-2351*

One of the most famous craftsmen in New England, he makes traditional baskets from ash in his home state of Maine. His name has national recognition; his work is signed and collectible. Large baskets cost from $800 upward.

Wood and Furniture

BOWER STUDIOS
Vergennes, VT; ☎ *802/877-6868*

Husband-and-wife team who created Archiblocks (blocks in architectural shapes and features) as well as furniture, screens, and things designed from architectural elements. They even have log-cabin birdhouses.

DAVIN AND KESSLER
Exeter, RI; ☎ *401/295-7515*

Small wooden accessories such as mirrors, knives, and letter openers in sleek, contemporary styles that take your breath away. Prices from $17 to $36.

THOMAS MOSER
Portland, ME; ☎ *207/774-3791*

Moser makes new Shaker-style furniture designs that are considered among the most important pieces in the genre; each is signed and considered collectible. We are talking megabucks for what will be the Gustav Stickley of tomorrow, in its own way. Available through your interior designer or in one of their New England showrooms.

PETER PETROCHKO
Oxford, CT; ☎ *860/888-9835*

Unbelievable containers and vessels that seem to float together as wooden mosaics; recipient of numerous prizes and awards; featured in crafts, travel, and home-decorating magazines.

WOODEN EWE/BILL & SUZANNE HALLET
Jefferson, ME; ☎ 207/549-3932. Yarmouth, ME; ☎ 207/846-6483

Rocking Rabbits, Batman! Original painted wooden rocking animals (an original design can be commissioned) fashioned after just about any beast you could imagine. Featured in major museums and FAO Schwarz, this is exactly the kind of thing you dream of buying for your child and keeping in the family for generations. Prices ranging from $150 to $300 seem inexpensive for what you get.

Pottery & Ceramics

GABRYL DESIGNS
Rumford, RI; ☎ 401/521-2830

Pet-perfect treasures in bowls, containers, picture frames, and wall plaques. The teapot with legs is a must-have. Almost everything is under $20.

JANE HILLMAN/WHITE DOG POTTERY
Easthampton, MA; ☎ 413/527-5665

Rabbits, flowers, or birds in pastels on sweet backgrounds. Has a country air that is sweet and childlike, yet avoids being cloying.

BRUCE LENORE
Providence, RI; ☎ 401/273-9728

One-of-a-kind abstract art pieces created from clay; raku fired.

SARAH MOTT
Attleboro, MA; ☎ 508/226-4785

The Nature Company was buying up a storm when we discovered this birdhouse craftsmaster at a show.

She does birdhouses, feeders, and baths . . . all from ceramics. Birdhouses begin at $75.

Potteries

For a list of Cape Cod potteries, see page 197.

EDGECOMB POTTERS
Rte. 27, Boothbay Harbor, ME; ☎ *207/882-6802*

They call themselves Maine's largest crafts gallery. All the country-style pottery is made here; they are famous for their glazes, especially the variations in shades of blue.

GREAT BARRINGTON POTTERY
Rte. 41, Housatonic, MA; ☎ *413/274-6259*

Richard Bennett creates earthenware pottery with a flavor more Japanese than American colonial. Just north of Great Barrington.

ROWANTREES POTTERY
Union St., Blue Hill, ME; ☎ *207/374-5535*

Earthenware with a three-dimensional design so the hollyberries or blueberries or mistletoe seem almost real. Also dinnerware with colored glazes and country looks.

SALMON FALLS POTTERY
Oak St., Dover, NH; ☎ *603/749-1467*

Although we aren't big on most styles of earthenware, we do like New England–style colonial pottery. It's usually taupe in color and painted with a simple design in cobalt. Salmon Falls sells first- and second-quality pieces in a location outside of Portsmouth, but convenient to your day trips and right near the Yield House Outlet. Your kids may enjoy watching the potters at work (while you shop). Open daily, 9am to 5pm.

SHEFFIELD POTTERY
Rte. 7, Sheffield, MA; ☎ 413/229-7700

This pottery is rather ordinary but makes good birth, wedding, and/or anniversary plates, which you can special order. They also sell some Pfaltzgraff. There is a good selection of crafts supplies for potters. Open Sundays.

WESLEYAN POTTERS
350 S. Main St., Middletown, CT; ☎ 860/347-5925

Actually a potter-and-weaver combo; their annual sale is held during the first 2 weeks in December. You are welcome to stop by any time Tuesday through Saturday.

Glass

KEER DESIGN
Central Falls, RI; ☎ 401/724-1224

Perfume bottles for collectors; colored glass in many varieties including cone-shaped vases that are sensational. Clean lines, quality color; modern glass with a message that whispers "collect."

SIMON PEARCE
Quechee, VT; ☎ 802/295-2711

Irish talent who came to Vermont and has since opened a chain of stores to sell his glass and crystal. Trained in Scandinavia at the big-name *glassverks.* Understated elegance and simplicity mark his work; his traditional values give you value for your money.

Jewelry

ROSS COPPELMAN
Yarmouthport, MA; ☎ 508/362-6108

Very interesting, intricate work that seems to combine Etruscan inspiration with precious and/or semiprecious stones.

JUDITH KAUFMAN
Farmington Valley Arts Center, Avon, CT; ☎ *203/678-0165*

Gold and gemstones worked together in fanciful designs with a hint of the ancient and spiritual translated in a dramatic, breathtaking fashion.

DIDI SUYDAM
Providence, RI; ☎ *401/331-5537*

Primitive design shapes meld with contemporary form to create gold or sterling jewelry that is both old and new—and therefore classical. Many pieces combine metal worked with stones.

CRAFTS GALLERIES

· ·

🛍 THE ARTFUL HAND
36 Copley Place, Boston, MA

Right smack in the middle of Boston's fanciest downtown mall is this good-sized crafts shop, which does a huge business in wedding gifts. All mediums are represented here, although glass and ceramics are the primary focus.

GALLERY 33
Market St., Portsmouth, NH

A small gallery in the main shopping part of town that is well stocked with pottery and whimsical ceramics, ideal for gifts or collectors.

SPECTRUM
Newport, Nantucket, etc.

A chain, if that's the right word. The shops represent the best of New England craftspeople in all mediums; about one-third of the collection is jewelry. They are usually located on the main shopping street and right in the thick of things. The type of store you can always rely on.

SUN-UP GALLERY
Between Westerly and Watch Hill on Rte. 1A

If you come to see one of America's most famous carousels in Westerly, Rhode Island, also take in the shopping scene—especially this gallery, which sells clothes, fiber arts, and other crafts.

VERMONT STATE CRAFT CENTER
Mill St., Frog Hollow, Middlebury, VT

This gallery for about 250 local craftspeople is located right near Frog Hollow, a part of town devoted to cute shops and those craftspeople with their own stores. Mecca for crafts aficionados. Visit both areas.

CRAFTY TOWN: NORTHAMPTON, MA

· ·

For the person looking for a quick overview of New England's best craftspeople, the person who can't get to a big juried fair and who is still looking for a travel adventure, there's no question but to head for Northampton, Massachusetts. Northampton happens to be about a 20-minute drive north of West Springfield, where the June ACC show is held, so you may want to plan to hit both. Besides, Northampton is the home of Smith College; it has a number of antiques shops and some good vintage-clothing sources. Also note that you are 15 to 20 minutes from five major colleges and from Deerfield Village (see page 99), and merely an hour from Sturbridge (see page 101) and Brimfield.

Main Street has a number of very nice stores and even a fresh and exciting minimall, but the real core of the retail scene is the crafts business—most of the galleries are on Main Street. Rumor has it that 1,500 professional craftspeople live and work in the valley around Northampton. When the ACC June fair comes to Springfield, the entire city of Northampton goes hog-wild and hosts Crafts Night. All the galleries are open, candles light the street, and wine flows. Northampton is the place to be.

There is a pamphlet published locally called *A Visitor's Guide to Galleries in Northampton*. Write: Greater Northampton Chamber of Commerce, 62 State St., Northampton, MA 01060, or call 413/584-1900.

Chapter Six

. . . .

NEW ENGLAND HOME

THE ENGLISH HOME GOES COLONIAL

. . . .

If there's one thing you will leave New England wanting to buy—the one thing to define your entire trip—it'll probably be a wagon. Yep, a wagon. If not a wagon, it'll be a carriage . . . or an old wooden wheelbarrow. Nothing says New England faster than a front yard decorated with an old wagon filled with flowering plants. This single contagious piece of style will leave town with you—if not in a crate to be shipped to your home, then to be carried as a memory of what makes New England special.

Part of New England's charm is not only its architectural styles, which meld together to form a patchwork of Americana, but its distinctly colonial marriage of need and art; the Shaker design heritage is nothing if not the personification of function as well as style. The Yankee arts and crafts we appreciate today are more a statement of a clever mind and a body in need than of a purely creative soul.

True, Boston was renowned for its craftspeople even before the Revolutionary War. But it's the countryside, much of which is now suburbia, that influenced what we today call "New England style." While Federal style is still big in the larger cities (and in New England), it is the elements of colonial style that give us the country look we love.

To familiarize yourself with these charming touches, pick up any of the myriad magazines and books that worship at the altar of milk paint. Mary Emmerling writes a series of books that focus on country styles; Mary Randolph Carter has written a few; Martha Stewart needs no introduction—her Christmas book is especially nice on New England touches.

But the best way to get ideas on how to incorporate New England's decorative touches into your own lifestyle is to see the houses and hotels in person. House tours are frequently conducted for charity events; many are hosted by local historical societies. More to the point, why do we associate New England charm with staying at an inn? Because we hope to absorb the design elements of country living by sleeping with them for a few nights. Country inns often use reproduction furnishings, but the better inns (i.e., the most expensive) spend their energy combining real antiques with appropriate finishing touches so that history can come alive in your guest room.

DICTIONARY OF NEW ENGLAND ELEMENTS

If you scope out enough houses (and yes, inns) you'll find that certain design elements will travel and translate to cities outside of New England, making them practical for any colonial- or country-style home. Much of what you see can even be combined with French-country and English-country looks for the same flavor.

Baskets

The first shopping carts were made of locally grown reed or wood. A well-made basket can last 100 years.

Birdhouse

The birdhouse has become the fashion statement of the 1990s—especially the weathered and old-looking birdhouse that was probably made yesterday but appears as if it were 50 years old. In the proper setting, one can combine birdhouses, weathervanes, and whirligigs and get away with it. But it takes talent.

Buckboard

Well, actually any old—and we mean *old*—carriage or wagon will do the trick. The point here is that it has to have the old country look; if painted, the paint must be weathered and flaked. The wagon should be filled with planted flowers—geraniums and petunias are just fine. Finally, the buckboard must be placed at a properly jaunty angle across the front yard or near the driveway so as to look natural . . . and charming.

Candles

Once the hot days of summer were gone, candle-dipping historically became the top priority, as this tedious and time-consuming project was imperative to prepare for the short days of winter. Pieces of string were dipped time after time to build up layers of wax. Bayberry became the most popular type of candle, because it didn't melt in summer like tallow and had a clean scent when burned.

Dyes

Natural dyes were used until the mid-1800s when chemicals from Europe changed the color of the very fabric of life. Today, fiber arts can still be dated by the type of dyes used in the fabric.

Garden

You've never seen so many nurseries in your life, especially in Cape Cod. The New England look celebrates the fact that the region has four distinct seasons by cultivating and displaying flowers for each.

Formal gardens are rare; a flourish of color that surrounds the house and welcomes the guest is not.

Glass

Used only for windows in the early years, glass dates back to the mid-1600s in this country, but did not become commonly used until the late 1700s and early 1800s, when technological advances made it possible to create moderately priced glass bottles, containers, and drinking glasses for the masses.

Hatboxes

Highly collectible today (and hard to find in good condition), the ideal hatbox (or bandbox) is lined in dated newspaper, which serves to authenticate your purchase. Wooden hatboxes were made in the late 1700s, but died out by the time of the Civil War. The Shelburne Museum has an excellent collection.

Hooked Rugs

A winter craft created to take advantage of leftover materials and form something warm for floorboards. Hooked rugs were created using flour sacks and wool remnants; the most popular ones depict houses or animals. It's rare to find a bird design other than an American eagle; half-circle rugs became popular only after 1870.

Paint

Colonial houses were wooden. While the Cape Cod look is defined by grayed and weathered shingles, most colonial homes are painted in color combinations that have been popular for centuries. While every paint company in the country makes appropriate colors, you may want to look at the Martha Stewart Dutch Boy colors created specifically for Kmart, and the Sturbridge paints marketed by Old

Sturbridge Village and sold in paint and decorating stores or by special order.

Pottery

Earthenware dishes and vessels were made in colonial times when metals were scarce and glass was not yet perfected. Stoneware was developed for durability, while soft-paste porcelain dishes usually came from England with transfers specifically designed for the American market.

Scrimshaw

Carved and/or etched ivory, traditionally created by sailors from whalebone.

Silhouette

Also called a profile, the silhouette was the photograph of the masses in times before Matthew Brady was even born. Itinerant artists cut the silhouette, usually in black paper, and mounted it on a white background. The more elaborate the cutting, the higher the value.

Tavern Signs/Trade Signs

Tavern signs, frequently worked in a three-dimensional fashion, were the first ads in this country and were soon followed by trade signs, which announced the location of the towns' crafts and service people. Often the design of the trade sign was the only indication of the quality of services rendered by its owner, so the sign was a status symbol as well as an advertisement.

Theorem

A still life created by stenciling a design onto a light velvet background. A proper activity for refined young ladies.

Tombstone

New England art at its most primitive . . . and we think best.

Weathervane

The crowning glory to any colonial home is the weathervane. Even if the house was built yesterday and the weathervane came from Korea (ours did), we're talking about style here. A proper weathervane is attached to a cupola. It won't do to stick your vane up there with a clamp. If your house does not have a cupola, you can buy one at any hardware store. They also sell them at roadsides here and there.

Whirligig

If you haven't got a weathervane (or a cupola), a whirligig will do. You probably shouldn't have both, as it would be a bit over-the-top style-wise and might be a giveaway that you haven't quite got Puritan in your blood. Whirligigs are wind machines, usually crafted of wood and painted bright colors, with a small propeller somewhere in the design. The wind turns the propeller, which powers the mechanisms in the design of your whirligig. The best ones are intricately animated: cows that can be milked by farmers, trout that can be landed by fishermen, etc.

Wreath

In most parts of the U.S., the wreath comes out at Christmastime. In New England, a wreath on the door is a sign of welcome throughout the year. The ribbon or decoration on the wreath, the composition of the wreath itself, changes with the seasons. But the wreath itself is a constant.

THE COLONIAL SCENE: HISTORIC DEERFIELD, MA

· ·

Historic Deerfield is a small blip on the side of the road that remains totally nontouristy and isolated from the commercial madness that affects so many other historic New England towns. Although real people do live in the town and kids really do go to Deerfield Academy, the Village almost feels like a movie set. It's quiet and perfect.

Deerfield boasts most of its action on the main street in town, although there are a few buildings, homes, and museums to explore on a side street or two. The main street in town is refreshingly named The Street. There really aren't any other streets in town anyway.

The town is basically a living museum. Twelve houses that are not populated are restored and open to the public; you buy one ticket that allows you admission to all the homes. Toward one end of town is the Deerfield Inn, where you can spend the night or just have a meal. There are a few shops on the main street, although Deerfield has no Gap, and no Banana Republic. We couldn't even spot a hardware store or barber shop. The town is exactly as it might have been in the 18th century. Pick up the Visitor's Map to see the layout of the whole town, stores included.

Another attraction of Deerfield is the surrounding area. Northampton (see page 91) is only about 20 minutes away and there are many other simple shopping pleasures on the rural roads nearby.

Finds

THE DEERFIELD INN
The Street, Deerfield, MA

If you are doing Deerfield right, you are staying at the Inn. You can stay in any of the charming nearby

Old Deerfield Craft Fair

An annual event held toward the end of September on the grounds of the Memorial Hall Museum, in Deerfield. This is a juried show with about 250 craftspeople from many states. This part of the U.S. is particularly known as a crafts capital. Call 413/774-7476 for the exact dates each year. Open 10am to 5pm, rain or shine.

towns (Amherst, Northampton) and drive here for a tour, but it will not feel the same. Few treats are as special as a walk down Main Street after dinner, or an early-morning stroll past historic houses.

The Deerfield Inn has two room rates, based on whether you eat dinner there or not. But there are no real bargains here. The Inn does include tea as part of the deal and children are welcome. Bed-and-breakfast prices are about $60 per person; with dinner included, prices are about $85 per person. There's an extra charge for kids in the room, cribs, etc. Some weekends have a 2-night minimum. Sometimes a carriage ride is thrown in. We admit to some of the nicest, most serene evenings in our lives spent walking around Deerfield before dinner at the inn. For reservations call 413/774-5587

Museum Store
The Street, Deerfield, MA

The store is in a house next door to the Inn; it has several rooms filled with museum-store goodies. There are reproductions of 18th-century crafts, many books, some children's gifts, and many decorative arts. Postcards too. This is an excellent museum store. Open 9:30am to 4:30pm.

MEMORIAL HALL MUSEUM
Memorial St., Deerfield, MA

There is a small museum store in the back. It is very different from the slick Museum Store, offering a funky blend of toys and crafts.

YANKEE CANDLE COMPANY
Rte. 5, South Deerfield, MA

Candle companies are a dime a dozen in New England, but this one is huge, has a nook that sells seconds, its own museum, a snack shop, and clean rest rooms. Really. You can also dip candles here—a sport your kids will adore. Open 9:30am to 5:30pm daily. For mail-order information call 800/243-1776. Although candles weigh a ton and are often packaged in breakable glass, they do make great gifts. In the seconds shop, you could get awfully good stuff for $10.

THE COLONIAL SCENE: STURBRIDGE, MA

Sturbridge may be known to every schoolchild and parent who has visited historic Old Sturbridge Village (often referred to as OSV), but it has been a hot spot since about 1729, when the first lead mine in the U.S. was opened. Over half a million tourists visit every year, but they don't give a hoot about the lead mine. They come for colonial history. They come to go shopping.

Route 20 is the main street as you pass through town to get to Old Sturbridge Village. It is populated with motels, restaurants, and stores. The oldest part of the town is actually off of Route 20 where The Publick House still stands (turn right on Route 131 from Route 20).

Finds

ANTIQUE CENTER
Yesterday's, Rte. 20, Sturbridge, MA

Upstairs over the Yesterday's restaurant, you'll find
one and a half floors of dealers (about 30) selling
colonial looks at moderate prices. Check your handbag in one of the wooden bins as you enter. Open
daily, 10am to 5pm.

OLD STURBRIDGE VILLAGE MUSEUM STORE
Sturbridge, MA

This is another great museum store, although we
are compelled to warn you that you can find some
of these goods elsewhere and for less money.
Sturbridge has the colonial theme so well orches-
trated that they even sell their own brand of paint—
and it's great paint. (There is also national distribution for this paint, so before you go schlepping
4 gallons home, check with your local hardware
store.) There are also stencils with instructions and
country-style gifts. You need not pay admission to
the Village to shop in the museum store.

RENOVATOR'S SUPPLY
Sturbridge Village, Sturbridge, MA

In the same group of shops as Country Curtains and
next door to Crabtree & Evelyn, Renovator's Supply is the retail showroom for the catalog of the
same name. They only have a few retail stores, so
this may be one of your only chances to see the goods
in person. The store has a nice colonial feel to it,
but is not much on charm or decor, considering we're
talking experts in renovation. Prices seem to be the
same as in the catalog. This is the place for old-style
new sinks, brass doorplates and doodads, taps, carpet rods, and whatever else you may need for renovation of your Victorian or colonial home.

STURBRIDGE MARKETPLACE
559 Main St. (Rte. 20), Sturbridge, MA

One of those semi-cute minimalls built into a renovated factory, this group of shops tries awfully hard, but doesn't quite cut it after you've seen the quality of goods at the Old Sturbridge Village Museum Store. Not bad if you are really curious, but don't give up time in Brimfield to shop here. The colonial look prevails in most of the shops.

STURBRIDGE YANKEE WORKSHOP
Main St. (Rte. 20), Sturbridge, MA

This is a great place if you are into inexpensive colonial repro furniture. We think it is a bit expensive for what it is, but the look is certainly there. Reminds us of Yield House, another New England firm. Open daily; Sunday from 11am to 5pm.

YANKEE CANDLE COMPANY
434 Main St. (Rte. 20), Sturbridge, MA

While your kids are being steeped in colonial history, don't let them miss this opportunity to dip their own candles. Open daily.

STURBRIDGE POTTERY
99 New Boston Rd., Sturbridge, MA

Earthenware with a raku style created by Gary and Ann Malone. Some pieces have colonial or Southwestern inspirations. Not far off Route 20.

YANKEE HOME STYLE
. . . .

If you are seriously into this, you must get a book called *Old House Catalog,* compiled by Lawrence Grow and published by Sterling/Main Street. We got ours at Mystic Seaport. The book consists of listings of suppliers for house renovations. You can also

write directly to Sterling Publishing Co., Inc., 387
Park Ave. S., New York, NY 10016.

FABRICS AND LINENS

· ·

Off-Pricers

For those who need fabrics, bed linens, towels, or
table linen, there are a number of New England
sources that offer a variety of price breaks.

Marshalls   With dozens of stores in New England,
Marshalls sells housewares and domestic linens at
prices that range from 20% to 50% off regular retail. There are so many Marshalls that you can call
them for the one nearest you (☎ 800/627-7425).

Linen Factory Outlets

Your best opportunity for a price break comes in
buying directly from the factory, although domestic
linen outlet stores are not traditionally among the
best of the outlet stores. Towels are easy to find, but
bed linen is rarely in the latest style or substantially
discounted.

Alpine Sheets & Towels   These aren't the most
come-hither of outlet stores, but if you get in there
and poke around you will find Fieldcrest at a discount. There's an outlet in Freeport, Maine.

Laura Ashley   Although basic design concepts come
from England, the sheets and towels are made in
the U.S. and a smallish selection is available in the
outlet store in Freeport, Maine.

Canon   Although they have a number of outlet
stores throughout New England, Canon has chosen
not to go into malls and usually has a freestanding
store on the edge of town. It often looks like a log
cabin and may not be too attractive. Don't be shy.

Polo/Ralph Lauren   All Ralph Lauren outlet stores
(New England locations include Kittery and
Freeport, ME; Manchester and North Conway, NH;

Clinton, CT; and Worcester, MA) have a domestic linens department; prices vary enormously, depending on the age of the goods. Often you will find the same merchandise featured in department stores; prices may be the same as white-sale department store days or better.

Springmaid/Wamsutta   Despite the fact that we've seen patterns we've liked from both these brands, the factory-outlet store (in Fall River, MA) we checked out was downright depressing: little merchandise, not much color or oomph, and little to covet.

Annual Sales

Just like in England, many design resources rely on a once- or twice-yearly house cleaning to make room for new styles and merchandise.

Pierre Deux   Their Boston sale is advertised and features the famous cotton fabrics in Provençal prints at a fraction of their usual cost. We paid $8 a yard for various prints; the sheet sets were also marked down to prices that made them almost reasonable.

FABRIC OUTLETS

While most of New England's famous mills have closed down, there are still some fabric outlet sources where big-time fabrics are sold for very good prices.

The Barn   We have mixed feelings about The Barn, since we have used this resource many times. The day we found the Gloria Vanderbilt floral print for $5 a yard, we thought the place was fabulous. The day they delivered the slipcover they made for us we were far from impressed. Fabric-wise, this store has a huge selection, and while they do a huge business in Waverly, there are better-quality fabrics to be had. The fabrics are housed in sections spanning a converted old barn, so wander around, up and down, and through to see everything. Located at 50 Herd Ave., Bridgeport, CT.

Osgood Mills   Known as the largest fabric source in the Northeast, this mill has a designer department with names like Waverly, Schumacher, and Kauffman, which does the milling for Clarence House. If you want a fabric they don't have, they will order it for you at 30% off retail. They sell current merchandise, not closeouts. Directly off Main Street at 30 Magaziner Place, Springfield, MA.

Seaport Fabrics   You will drive right by this resource on your way to Mystic Seaport; it's your loss if you don't stop and check it out. All the big names in fabric are carried here, from Waverly to Brunsweig. Discounts vary depending on the quality and age of the fabric. The people here are knowledgeable and will help you match up your swatches. Route 27 is the main street in town; the store is next to the Mobil gas station.

WALL COVERINGS/WINDOW TREATMENTS

Country Curtains   This chain of curtain shops is always located in a restored house and sells a wide range of country and colonial looks at moderate prices. They also sell Claire Murray Nantucket hooked rugs, some decorative arts, curtain rods, and other assorted needs for the house. While merchandise can be bland, the surroundings are often spectacular. Call 800/456-0321 to find the shop nearest the location you are visiting.

London Lace   Lace curtains for your colonial or country home. Located at 167 Newbury St., Boston, MA.

Rue de France   This is where you buy country-style lace curtains or runners, ready-made or by the yard. Although they are French, the curtains are a huge hit in American colonial homes. Great mail-order business. At 215 Newbury St., Boston, MA.

CHINA AND HOUSEWARES

Alessi Yes, you can buy a teapot at a slight discount in this tiny shop that isn't really an outlet, but marks down Italian designer housewares. Downstairs at Howland Place in New Bedford, MA.

China Fair Warehouse I only went here because Ronnie Scharlack insisted; from the outside we were not impressed. Inside you find a jungle of goods, especially from Copco. This is the kind of store that separates the princesses from the serious shoppers. There are a few branch stores in the Boston area; check out the one at 70 Needham St. in Boston.

Corning/Revere I grew up with copper-bottom Revere Ware; you can still buy it—and it's modestly priced—at the outlet stores, along with all sorts of gadgets, cooking aids, glasswares, and essentials.

Crate and Barrel With many retail stores and a few outlet stores around New England, Crate and Barrel is similar to Pottery Barn and offers a clean design look at moderate prices. The outlet gives you a great opportunity to find gifts or finishing touches for your own home. Located at 711 Huron Ave., Cambridge, MA. Other outlets in Clinton, Connecticut, and Kittery, Maine.

Dansk Although Dansk is most famous for their colored enamel cookware, they also have a wide range of housewares. Some stores are in mall cities (Kittery, Maine), others are freestanding.

Kitchen Etc. This resource sells a variety of makes of dishes from the houses that don't have their own outlet stores (Noritake, Pfaltzgraff) as well as glassware, knives, and the kitchen and baking necessities we prefer to buy at discount. They even carry Calphalon, the pricey cookware many professionals swear by. There are four New England locations: for more information or to order their catalog call 800/232-4070.

Lenox   Their own factory-outlet stores feature their dishes and glasswares. We particularly like the outlet in Kittery, Maine.

Reed & Barton   They, too, have an outlet in Kittery, Maine; a good source for gifts, as well as silver and everyday wares.

Ross Simmons   Call 800/556-7376 this very minute to get good prices on silver, dinnerware, and dishes. This discount firm does business all over the country from their New England headquarters and often has the best prices in town. Before a trip to the outlet, call them and scribble down prices (and shipping costs) so you know what makes a sale worthwhile when you hit the outlets. One of our china patterns cost less here than in England. They also sell fine jewelry and have a catalog. Located at 9 Ross Simmons Dr., Cranston, RI.

Royal Doulton   Many outlets all over America selling dishes, porcelain gift items, baby sets, Toby mugs, glassware, and even telephones.

Villeroy & Boch   With outlet stores in mall cities (Kittery, Maine) and on their own (Norwalk, Connecticut), Villeroy & Boch feature great buys on their famous china patterns as well as various crystal and gift items.

Wedgwood   Although shops currently sell both Wedgwood and Waterford, these two companies will be separating their marketing efforts. There aren't a lot of outlet stores (there is one in Kittery, Maine), but you can find a fair selection of designs and prices that compare to those in England.

REPRODUCTIONS

There is a very fine line between what is antique (by government standards, anything over 100 years old), what is old, what is junk, what is repro, and what is simply fake. Furthermore, many stores sell a combination of all these things arranged in such splendor that an uneducated eye cannot tell one from the next. Our rule of thumb is you get what you pay for. Education is the key to bargaining power. It's also safe to assume you'll pay less for real antiques when you shop out of season and in out-of-the-way places. It is safe to assume that antiques dealers are scouting the same areas you are. Museum-quality works are very, very hard to come by these days. You'll want an expert to help you shop if your aim is to impress the Rockefellers. If you want the look for less, you might want to try some sources of reproduction furniture:

Sturbridge Yankee Workshop; Main Street (Route 20), Sturbridge, MA: A great place if you are into inexpensive colonial repro furniture.

Thomas Moser; Cobbs Bridge Road, New Gloucester, ME: The leading craftsman of important, expensive Shaker repro.

Yield House; North Conway, NH: We're not that keen on the quality here; we think the price is a bit high for what you get. However, prices are still in the moderate range and it has the quality of all new American furniture these days (which is why we like old furniture). Their look is very colonial and they offer everything from sofas to table arts. Many items come in assemble-yourself form. Call 800/258-4720 for a free catalog and information on their freestanding stores and outlets.

Chapter Seven

· · · · · · · · · ·

CONNECTICUT & RHODE ISLAND

WELCOME TO CONNECTICUT

· ·

I live and work in Connecticut; we chose it over every other state when we decided to leave California, to hit the East Coast, and to move someplace where the leaves change colors.

To us, Connecticut offers a combination of many worlds. You're close to New York, not far from Boston, and yet very much a part of colonial America and the New England lifestyle. We've got the sea and the seasons. The leaves are gorgeous. And so is the shopping, in its own, low-key way.

If you're visiting the area, you won't need a guide-book to Connecticut as much as you'll need a subscription to one of the small-town newspapers that can keep you posted as to sales, auctions, community news, and retail happenings. When you find your favorite town, buy the local newspaper for subscription information.

Of course, we have more than tag sales. There are tons of antiques stores, from the fanciest New York dealers who gave up the city and moved to the country, to flea markets and fun sales that come and go. We've also gotten our own world-class outlet situation. I call it a situation because a new mall has moved in a few miles from an older outlet mall and together they give you one of the biggest wallops a discount shopper can get.

You might think that Connecticut is just a sub-urb of New York, but shoppers who come this way will soon find we've got a lot more to offer. Come on up.

THE LAY OF THE LAND

In my mind, there are two Connecticuts: the coast, which stretches from New York to Rhode Island, and inland—which is much more traditional, more rural and a tad more New England-y.

Fairfield County is the southwestern-most county of Connecticut, with New York State on its western border and Long Island Sound on its southern border. This is the gold coast of Connecticut—known for its wealthy folks. Much of Fairfield County is indeed a bedroom community to Manhattan, but how "suite" it is. Not only do you have your choice of several storybook villages to explore and shop, but you also have the beach. And, going a little further along the coast, you have Yale and then Outlet Heaven, right off good old I-95.

Inland, the state stretches from New York to Massachusetts, with country towns filled with antiques shops and traditional New England treats.

Like tag sales. Fairfield County is famous for the quality of its tag sales. Martha Stewart, who has lived in Fairfield County for many years, claims in her books (and magazine) that much of the wonderful stuff she pictures comes from these very tag sales. And, of course, it only costs pennies. For more on tag sales, see page 65. Then pack your bags and head to Connecticut.

GETTING AROUND

For getting inland, Hartford's international airport (Bradley Field) makes arriving and departing Connecticut a breeze.

If you want to visit the coast, you may prefer to use New York airports or the Providence airport. Commuter trains and Amtrak arrive from New York and Boston areas. While you can enjoy a few communities traveling by train, you will need a car if you are exploring . . . or doing the tag sales.

Driver's tip: While I-95 is one of the most famous highways in America, and it skirts the coast of Connecticut brilliantly, I very often go to Boston by heading across to Hartford (north on I-91), then taking I-84 East until you connect with I-90, which is a toll road and well worth it. That's to say, it doesn't have the large number of trucks you'll get on I-95.

If you want to pick up I-95 again north of Boston, do so via I-495 North. I use I-95 for getting to Cape Cod, Newport, or when I am driving alone and want the security of heavier traffic.

SLEEPING IN CONNECTICUT
. . . .

Hartford is the state capital and Stamford is the hub of Fairfield County—the part of Connecticut closest to Manhattan. Each has a handful of nationally known hotel chains; there is a string of motels on the way to the airport outside of Hartford, and there's a Sheraton right downtown; we stay there often. (Corporate rate, $109 per night!) Stamford is a lot more glamorous with a Sheraton, a Hyatt Regency, and a Marriott.

New Haven, an old colonial city, has a Holiday Inn and a Howard Johnson (among other choices). I don't think many tourists stay in New Haven, but you never know.

Mystic, a big tourist destination, has its share of representatives from the major chains, but our regular here is the Mystic Hilton (see page 131). Inns and other motels are plentiful. It pays to do some research to plan your nightly accommodations. There are some country inns here and there, and there's a famous spa in Norwich, but for family travel, we usually book with one of the big chains.

GREENWICH

. . . .

The serious shopping territory for all of Fairfield County is Stamford, where there is a large and famous regional mall with duplicates of New York's finest shops. This said, you can understand that Greenwich—nestled between Stamford and the New York state boundary—is a hub city of a totally different sort.

Greenwich has an amazing amount of retail in an old-fashioned, small-town sense, and serves not only Greenwich, but the enclave of other towns in the area, including Old Greenwich, Cos Cob, and Riverside. Greenwich has recently opened its own **Saks Fifth Avenue**—a new concept for Saks called Main Street Store—and is far more rich and hip and with-it than any old mall could ever be. Step this way.

There is main-street shopping aplenty in "downtown" Greenwich, after which you can head out on Route 1 (Putnam Avenue) and stop at a few consignment and/or antiques shops. While many of these shops are pricey (this is Greenwich, after all), we've fallen into several bargains and had plenty of nice shopping days in a city that feels a little bit like England to us . . . with the added treat that you can spy a small patch of the Long Island Sound as you shop.

The Lay of the Land

The main street in Greenwich is called Greenwich Avenue; the stores make up the historically preserved district. This makes for some unusual architecture and a strange blend of wider-than-usual streets with more landmarks, monuments, and stone churches along them than in the average small town. This is not a typical New England village, but almost a Hollywood set for small-town America.

There's plenty of "real-people" business with the local pet stores, movie theaters, greengrocers, and lobstermen, along with a ton of cafes and bistros. Mostly you'll find downtown Greenwich an odd combination of 1950s retailing still going strong, 1980s Wall Street retailing still hanging in, and 1990s discount shopping thriving. How many other main streets in America have a magnificent freestanding **Polo/Ralph Lauren** shop across the street from a **Dress Barn?**

Greenwich Avenue crosses Putnam Avenue to offer even more shopping possibilities. Greenwich Avenue has three or four blocks of dense shopping, making this a longer than usual main street. Most noticeable is the fact that Greenwich does not have stoplights, so that uniformed police officers are stationed on each corner of Greenwich Avenue.

After you've shopped both sides of Greenwich Avenue, you'll want to check out Putnam Avenue— one side has a sprinkling of antiques shops, the other side has some fancy retail, some branches of the big chains, and some smaller, more specialized shops, perfect for those with time and money.

Finds

SAKS FIFTH AVENUE
205 Greenwich Ave., Greenwich

This is a small (35,000 sq. ft.) store, created by Saks as the prototype of what they call their Main Street Shops. Look for one to join the main shopping street of any of America's upscale–zip-code shopping districts. Like Greenwich.

The store has been carefully tailored to the local lifestyle. There's another Saks not far away in Stamford (a 20 minute drive) and of course, the flagship is on Fifth Avenue in Manhattan. But this store gives

you a quick fix on what Greenwich is all about—
discreet elegance and sporty chic with an emphasis
on designer bridge lines and designer accessories.

April Cornell
272 Greenwich Ave., Greenwich

The very best store in Greenwich when it comes to
exciting merchandise that you haven't seen before.
Cornell mixes clothing and home furnishings with
standard country looks à la Pierre Deux or Ralph
Lauren. The clothing, bed and table linens, and accessories come from India, but aren't that cheap
madras we remember from the 1960s. Instead you'll
see giant cabbage roses and looks that will remind
you of Kenzo, Yves Saint Laurent, and Pierre Deux
all at once. Prices are moderate to high, but twice
a year they have sales that are worth planning to
attend.

Late-night shopping is on Thursday when the
store stays open until 8pm; Sunday hours are noon
to 5pm.

Irresistibles
355 Greenwich Ave., Greenwich

This is a growing New England chain, begun in
Boston, with stores wherever there are people with
money—which is particularly interesting because the
clothes are not expensive or fancy, simply attractive
and moderately priced. There are some similarities
to Ann Taylor, but there's an emphasis on knitted
sweaters with designs and sort of preppy casual
clothes.

Just Books
19 East Putnam Ave., Greenwich

The perfect small-town bookstore honed to the tastes
of locals—that means along with best-sellers you
get books on gardening, entertaining, design, etc.

One of the best bought little stores we've seen in years. You'll feel rich and pampered and very Greenwich just by browsing.

E.L.D.C. Thrift Shop
Rte. 1, Cos Cob

Once you're headed north on East Putnam Avenue, you're headed for the consignment shops, where the Greenwich crowd sheds its cares. This store has some furniture and knickknacks, but concentrates on clothing; I once found the perfect Brooks Brothers bathrobe for $10. The exact same style was on sale at the Stamford Brooks Brothers, marked down from $169 to $135. I've also done well on cashmere sweaters for $30. However, last trip—*nada*. That's how it goes with this kind of shopping.

Estate Treasures
1162 Post Rd., Riverside

The most famous of the Greenwich consignment shops, this large shop is on the outskirts of town, where it packs tons of big pieces of furniture, some lamps, jewelry, and paintings into a shop brimming with light and the promise of a find. Alas, while the merchandise is top-drawer, the prices are seriously over-the-top.

NORWALK

Norwalk sprawls all over the waterfront and has many parts to it—each different. While it is not great as a retail haven, its sprawl has grown up around a lot of factories and there is a healthy outlet business here. There are no fabulous outlet malls, mind you; there's nothing serious to make a special trip to visit, but nevertheless there are bargains and good times to be had.

The Lay of the Land

South Norwalk: There's an absolutely adorable downtown renovation area called SoNo (kind of the SoHo of South Norwalk). The main street, Washington Street, isn't very long, but the cafes and stores are mighty cute. You can get off the Metro North train at South Norwalk and walk around.

East Norwalk: Stay on the train one more stop and you're in East Norwalk, home of a small outlet center (see page 56), which is easy to get to for those without cars who may be coming from New York. The bargains at **Dooney & Bourke** handbags will make the trip worth your time.

Norwalk Center: Norwalk Center is a little bit of a downtown area that has more shops; many of them discount or off-price. There are streets stretching out from **Norwalk Center** with their share of retailing, as well as the Lockwood-Matthews Mansion for sightseeing and an occasional antiques fair. It's next door to **Loehmann's** and the **Villeroy & Boch Outlet Store.**

Finds

DECKERS
692 West Ave. (Rte. 1), Norwalk

Worth the drive for men's, women's, and kids' discounts on very high-end merchandise, including Ralph Lauren. Sometimes advertises in Sunday's *New York Times.*

STEW LEONARD'S
100 Westport Ave. (Rte. 1), Norwalk

The infamous tourist attraction of the area, Stew Leonard's is the largest dairy store in the country. They sell milk, fruit and veggies, and other products (great butcher), but they are not simply a regular grocery store. When you see the petting farm and the animatronic cows that sing and dance, you'll see what we mean. You need a car to get here—it's halfway between Norwalk Center and Westport. Or you may arrive on one of the many tour buses. Bring the family—this place is a once-in-a-lifetime shopping extravaganza.

🛍 EXPOSURES CATALOG OUTLET OUTLET
41 S. Main St., Norwalk

Exposures is one of my favorite catalogs—the goods mostly pertain to photography and the showcasing of photographs, be it in frames, albums, screens, shadow boxes, or the like. The prices are fair to high, so the outlet store, where prices are low to fair, is much more fun. Closed on Sundays.

RIDGEFIELD

Ridgefield is one of those New England towns that has a main street lined with giant houses and two or three churches with appropriate steeples. The architecture ranges from pre-Revolutionary to Victorian; many of the homes have been turned into museums or inns. No matter how many times we drive this row, it still knocks us out.

The main-street shopping is not the kind that wows you, at least not at first glance. There are everyday, "real-people" shops and services here, but there are no branch stores of The Gap or Banana Republic. Instead, nestled here and there—right on and just off of Main Street—are a fair number of consignment shops, antiques stores, and pleasant shopping experiences.

The Lay of the Land

Ridgefield covers a tremendous amount of territory and stretches from a corner of Connecticut right to a corner of New York, so some people like to combine a trip here with a visit to Katonah, New York for even more antiques. There are three distinct shopping areas to Ridgefield: the junction of Routes 7 and 102, Main Street and its offshoots, and Copps Hill Common.

After shopping the antiques stores at the junction of Routes 7 and 102, follow Route 102 (Branchfield Road) for several miles until you dead-end right into Ridgefield's Main Street. When you get to Main Street (Route 35), turn right. Follow signs to public parking or park on Main Street.

Finds

ATTIC TREASURES
58 Ethan Allen Hwy. (Rte. 7), Ridgefield

Across the street from The Tag Sale Shop, the name really says it all. It's not as dusty as an attic, but it has the same possibilities. Most of the objects are dishes or glassware, but there's a good bit of other stuff too. When there's a sale on, you can do rather well. First-rate fun for those who like affordable antiques.

COUNTRY INTERIORS
3¹/₂ Cattonah St., Ridgefield

This is actually a design studio, but they are so good at the American-country look that you may want to look at the pieces they have for sale in the showroom—mostly chairs and finishing touches. Cattonah Street is right off Main Street, walking distance from your other shopping. Open Tuesday through Saturday, 11am to 4pm.

DEJA VU
23 Cattonah St., Ridgefield

Perhaps my favorite used-merchandise shop in Ridgefield because the prices are so good and the atmosphere is just so much fun. The store is not large, but is crammed with decorative items and clothing as well as a small amount of jewelry and accessories. It's better than a tag sale (for selection) and prices are less than at the other two consignment/antiques stores in town.

HAY DAY
21 Governor St., Ridgefield

There is another Hay Day in Westport, but this is the fancier of the two—the snazzy Victorian-style store is really a dressed-up farm stand that also sells gourmet foods. Don't forget a pack of the lemon sugar cookies. Open Monday through Saturday, 8am to 7pm; Sunday, 8am to 6pm.

VILLAGE EMPORIUM
384 Main St., Ridgefield

Country-style emporium crammed full of collectibles, stuff, repro and antiques—I found something for $10 that I'd seen at a tag sale the same day for $5, but that's show business. Big collection of teddy bears. Great fun. Open daily, 11am to 5pm.

HUNTER'S CONSIGNMENTS
426 Main St., Ridgefield

The entrance is actually in the parking area right off Main Street; the store is around the corner from The Silk Purse. Although the two consignment shops are rather similar, Hunter's seems a little more expensive to us and less likely to have a hidden treasure. But we have bought here before and continue to look.

C. DEVENS
446 Main St., Ridgefield

More consignments! Smaller shop, rather hoity-toity and not at all junky.

CONSIGNMENTS BY VIVIAN
458 Main St., Ridgefield

Yes! Whoever you are Viv, you're my gal. Vintage clothing and accessories, used clothing, antiques, fun stuff, great taste.

T. L. BENNETT
448 Main St., Ridgefield

The most heavenly divine European linen collection—at affordable prices.

THE SILK PURSE
470 Main St., Ridgefield

This is a consignment shop right on Main Street. It's rather large and has several aisles of tables and chairs, as well as some shelves in the back for dishes and an area for bedsteads. Prices are usually fair—not dirt cheap, but appropriate for the quality of the merchandise. Another shop in New Canaan, at 118 Main St.

THE RED PETTICOAT
113 West Lane (Rte. 35), Ridgefield

Isolated from the rest of town, The Red Petticoat is famous enough to include in your spree. The house predates the Revolutionary War; the name comes from the fact that the lady of the household used to hang out a red petticoat on the wash line as a signal to Revolutionary troops. Today, the house is filled with furniture and some decorative pieces in the pricey-to-serious range. This is on Route 35 in the opposite direction of Copps Hill.

RIDGEFIELD ANTIQUES CENTER
Copps Hill Common, Rte. 35, Ridgefield

Although there are 24 different dealers represented here, the space is not divided into cubbyholes or stalls, but is, in fact, quite roomy. You'll find the usual range of country-style items, from furniture with a European feel to quilts, dishes, silver,

Fiestaware, and jewelry. They do have sales. To get here, follow Main Street until it forks, then follow the right-hand fork, which is clearly marked as Route 35. It's not far from there. While you're at Copps Hill, check out a few of the other stores including **The Ridgefield General Store and Cafe.**

THE TAG SALE SHOP
Rte. 7, Ridgefield

You have to be feeling strong for a foray into this shop, as the merchandise is piled so deeply and densely that you're never sure what you've seen. There are lots of lamps and pieces of china and trays and small objects, and bottles and glasses and just things! Prices are low, but the junk factor is high.

LITCHFIELD

. . . .

If I were writing a book or doing a photo essay on classic New England towns, or entertaining people from international destinations—Litchfield would be one of the cities I'd insist on. It's just picture perfect.

The retail scene is not terrific and the social scene is extraordinarily trendy—check out the big-money New Yorkers dressed in head-to-toe Ralph Lauren and Cole-Haan mocs out walking their matching West Highland terriers. Look past them and you'll see a beautiful town green, some wonderful white houses with white picket fences (just like in post-cards), and a few fun-to-browse stores.

The Lay of the Land

Stores on the main street do not have addresses. Their business cards simply state "On the Green," and they are referred to in the same manner.

Litchfield and Kent (see below) are two points of a triangle that includes New Preston (see page

75), and the three towns can be included in one pleasant driving trip.

Also note there's a small town called Bethlehem 8 miles south of Litchfield on Route 63—it's a cutie-pie town that is especially friendly in fall and before Christmas. **The Christmas Shop** (18 East St.) is a dream come true. This is also the territory made famous by **White Flower Farm,** a nursery, not a flower stand.

Finds

THE CORNER STORE
Cobble Court, Litchfield

Located in Cobble Court, a small courtyard of stores behind the main shopping street, this tiny store is part toys, part sophisticated games of wonder—like computerized chess and books of mazes. Also some art supplies and needlework kits.

HAYSEED
On the Green, Litchfield

Whimsical blend of funny T-shirts, cards, bath soaps, jewelry, and country-style clothing.

D. W. LINSLEY ANTIQUES
Rte. 202, 499 Bantam Rd., Litchfield

Located outside Litchfield in a strip center, this is one fancy antiques store. Although it looks standard from the outside, once you enter you'll find an upstairs, a downstairs, and a handful of back rooms—all filled with country furniture. There are a few decorative items (many of these are repro) but the main business is big pieces of furniture with fairly big prices. Even if you don't buy, you owe it to yourself to see one of the best stores in the area.

THE LITCHFIELD EXCHANGE
Cobble Court, Litchfield

Also in Cobble Court, this small but packed store sells handmade items. We bought a basket here ($42), but there were quilts and other crafts at fairly good prices.

White Flower Farm
Rte. 63, Litchfield

Take Route 63 South (clearly marked at the Village Green in downtown Litchfield), and just a few miles out of town you'll get to one of New England's most famous (and expensive) nurseries. They have a mail-order business and are open seasonally from mid-April through October. Over 40 acres of field for you to wander in wonder.

Workshop
On the Green, Litchfield

Two-level store with ready-to-wear for women on the street level, and housewares—in the chic country mode, of course—downstairs.

R. Derwin Clothier
West and Meadow sts., Litchfield

Discount cashmere sweater?!! Not cheap, but better than full price. Then go next door to West Street Grill.

Barnidge & McEnroe
7 West St., Litchfield

Old-fashioned bookstore; crammed and spread over three floors and much fun.

KENT

One of Connecticut's most famous cutie-pie towns, Kent is mobbed on weekends and seriously, uncomfortably mobbed on leaf-season weekends. This is the typical one-lane town with adorable stores on Main Street. Everyone's fantasy begins here.

The Lay of the Land

You'll get to Kent on Route 7. You can't miss it; the road goes right through town. If you are connecting from Litchfield to Kent (or vice versa) take Route 63 North from Litchfield to Goshen, then Route 4 South to Route 7; follow Route 7 to Kent. Sundays are big days for strolling and shopping; stores are open from noon until 5pm.

Finds

THE CORNER SHOP
8 N. Main St., Kent

One of our favorite shops in Kent (aside from the ice-cream store) is the consignment shop, where prices range from fair ($18 for a good tole tray) to silly ($500 for a Kaffe Fassett sweater knitted from a kit). The store is so cute and has such nice merchandise, it's hard to believe that it's a consignment shop.

FOLKCRAFT INSTRUMENTS
Main St., Kent

Seems like a fancy music store, but they do sell a few high-priced instruments, the likes of which are not readily seen elsewhere.

WESTPORT
· ·

Westport has changed dramatically in the years that we have lived here and even changed tremendously in the last two years. The adorable and personable Main Street has been given over to the big-name branch stores of American retail so that as charming as it is, it does look a lot like an outdoor mall.

Should you care to stop at **The Limited, Laura Ashley, Banana Republic, The Gap, Gap Kids, Ann Taylor, Country Roads, Britches, Talbots,** or the like—now's your chance. **Barney's** has already come and (according to gossip) gone; rumor is that **Saks** will soon be moving in!

As one of the major commuter hubs in Fairfield County, Westport has a tremendous amount of special-event retailing. Check in the local newspaper, the *Westport News,* to find out if it's time for **Bargain Fest** (a flea market), the crafts show, or an antiques show. Tag sales are a regular weekend specialty. There's also a whole lot of consignment shops and antiques shops, fit for every taste and budget.

The Lay of the Land

Westport actually has two main drags. Main Street—you know, the one that looks like a mall—runs perpendicular to Route 1, The Boston Post Road. The Post Road (as it's called) stretches across the length of the town leading from Norwalk (see page 116) and **Stew Leonard's** (page 117), past the **Pepperidge Farm** headquarters (where you can smell the bread baking in the morning), over the Saugatuck River, past Main Street, and off toward the city of Fairfield. These are the two basic shopping areas. Between these two areas, you'll get to most of the stores you need. Tag sales are at home, so you'll need the local paper and a map (free from any real-estate office) in order to get to the homes.

Finds

AMERICAN HAND
125 Post Rd., Westport

Nestled off the street in a gray building that is part of a strip development, this crafts shop is one of the best in the area. They fly a flag out front to help you find the place.

LOCAL FARM STANDS

A & J's Farm Stand
1680 Post Rd. E., Westport

On the way to Fairfield, and very different from the Double L (see below), this simple country stand sells the best corn on the cob that I have ever eaten. Fresh tomatoes, zinnias, and this and that. Not fancy but everything here is of great quality.

Double L Stand
3 Kings Hwy. N., Westport

Farm stand, Christmas-tree headquarters, and multiseason shop full of the country spirit. Closes after Christmas until spring veggies come in. In spring and summer there are veggies as well as plants and flowers. Some home-baked goods, coffee, and gourmet foodstuffs; seasonal hot-dog stand. The Double L means Lloyd and Leslie—he runs the food part; she has a cutie-pie store in a stone house to the rear of the property where New England gifts and antiques are sold.

Lillian August
17 Main St., Westport

One of Westport's leading lights, major talents, and key retailers on Main Street, keeping it from becoming a total washout as a mall of been-there, done-that stores. At last, something original that you're gonna love.

This home-decorating shop is unique in the way it combines English country looks and quasi–Ralph Lauren looks for something that feels exactly right for a Connecticut Yankee. Ask about her sales, including her warehouse sale.

📑 HENRY LEHR HOME
19 Main St., Westport

Does Lillian August one better.

📑 ED MITCHELL'S
670 Post Rd. E., Westport

This is a great store, not just because of the clothes that are sold here, but because of the store's understanding of what retail used to be and the way the family works with the community. This is an old-fashioned haberdashery, where men and women can buy weekend and business clothes. They do a huge business in **Ralph Lauren** and other upscale names. Twice a year they have a huge tent sale, give out popcorn and hot dogs, and sell off goodies at low prices. They may have a warehouse clearance sale every now and then as well: Watch the local paper.

OUTLET HEAVEN

I don't know how to define this stretch of no-man's land other than to call it Outlet Heaven, a few exits off I-95 that will lead you to two factory-outlet malls. I'm talking about driving past New Haven, to Exits 63 and 65.

Finds

WESTBROOK FACTORY STORES
Exit 65 off of I-95, Westbrook

You can see part of the mall from the highway but you can't really see how to get there, so you exit, and turn left (if you are headed north on I-95) and then you cross over the highway and are on Flat Rock Place where in a few hundred yards you'll see a sign that says Westbrook Factory Stores. You turn left at the sign and drive for what seems to be some distance and you are beginning to doubt me. Keep on trucking; **J. Crew** lies up ahead.

So, finally you get there and you can't believe your eyes: the world's cutest little outlet mall, sort of done up like a Victorian train station. There are maybe 50 stores. Shopping hours are Monday through Saturday, 10am to 9pm, and Sunday, 11am to 6pm.

There are several big names here, but the best are **J. Crew, Osh Kosh b'Gosh, Timberland,** and **Rockport.**

CLINTON CROSSING PREMIUM OUTLET MALL
Exit 63 off of I-95, Clinton

This is another small outlet mall, about 60 stores, also very cute and very classy and with even more upscale tenants, including **Off Fifth,** the Saks Fifth Avenue outlet, **The Cosmetics Company** (Estee Lauder's outlet store), **Polo/Ralph Lauren, Episode, Malo Cashmere,** and many more.

MYSTIC

Mystic is the perfect destination, the perfect stop-over: It's halfway between New York and Boston. It manages to have tons of shops and an air of commercial success without feeling contrived or tacky. It's old-fashioned and it's inspirational—especially when you see the factory outlets. The outlets aren't that great, but they're fun and add an extra dimension to time spent in the area.

Located on the Connecticut coast, Exit 90 off of I-95, not too far from the Rhode Island state line, Mystic can be a weekend in itself or a pure shopping spree. Also check out nearby Stonington for antiques.

While Mystic is not normally mentioned in the same breath as colonial villages like Sturbridge and Deerfield, Mystic Seaport itself is several villages in one. The town tourist shopping mall (**Olde Mystick Village**) is a separate colonial village and then the two-part outlet resources make up yet another village. Mystic is a real down-home kind of place. The rich commercial past of this Connecticut port continues into its future . . . so bring your credit cards.

The Lay of the Land

Everything is easily at hand, but not within walking distance. The outlets are in two different strip centers, not visible from each other, so follow the arrows once you are in the parking lot to get from one to the other.

You can take the Mystic Trolley shuttle between the Seaport, downtown, some restaurants, and the Carousel Museum. It costs $2 per person for on/off access.

If there is a real downtown Mystic, it's on the other side of the river, closer to Groton, and it boasts the **Mystic River Antiques Center,** 14 Holmes Ave.; in it are 30 dealers, open daily year-round, 10am to 5pm.

Warning: Crowds can be fierce, especially on summer weekends. If it's hot, temperatures rise. Remember, Mystic is a major tourist attraction.

However, Mystic is divine out of season; try it in fall through Christmas and you won't be sorry. Mystic Seaport is open year-round. There are holiday promotions galore.

You can arrive in Mystic via Amtrak; there is a station in Old Mystic. There is also a trolley bus that connects the Seaport, Aquarium, mall, motels, downtown, etc. You can do this adventure without a car, but we don't recommend it.

Sleeping in Mystic

We invariably spend the night in Mystic. We've tried several of the motels, since the area is full of them, but have settled on paying a little more and enjoying the Mystic Hilton, which comes in at about $100 per night. It has a pool, it's next to the outlets, it's across from the Mystick Village mall and down the street from Steak Loft, where we always eat dinner.

Mystic Hilton
20 Coogan Blvd., Mystic

A modern structure with plenty of amenities, including its own branch of the gift shop from Mystic Seaport. There are assorted weekend rates, promotional deals for different times of the year, etc. There's no charge for children, regardless of age, when they share a room with their parents. Call 800/HILTONS or 860/572-0731; fax 860/572-0328.

Finds

Mystic Factory Outlets
Clara Dr., Mystic

There are two completely different strip centers that are known as MFO (Mystic Factory Outlets) I and II, and they are near each other, but not adjacent. Just go to the Mystic Hilton and then follow the signs in the parking lot, as the outlets share part of the Hilton's parking real estate.

These aren't the greatest outlets, considering how near you are to the big time (see page 129), but they're worth a look.

Mystic Seaport Museum Store
Mystic Seaport

Mystic Seaport does have some stores within the grounds of the park and you will enjoy them (as will your kids), but shopping aficionados will go nuts for the official museum store, which is at the main gate (South Gate). You can enter the store without paying admission to the park. Two floors feature 12 different categories of goods including important crafts (a pine-needle lightship basket at $3,800), nautical books, charts, foods, candies, and inexpensive gifts. You can get a 2-year subscription to their catalog for $1.

The Secret of Stonington

I almost hate to tell you about Stonington because it's one of those New England villages that really is perfect and you don't want it ruined. Especially since it's so close to Mystic, you know that there's a potential to go touristic and ballistic. Right now, it's a town that stretches right to the sea, with antiques shops lining the way. The stores don't open until 11am, so don't rush over first thing in the morning. There are no Sunday hours!

The main street is called Water Street (it leads to the water); don't miss **Quimper Faience,** the tons of antiques shops, or the chance to eat lobster at Skipper's. All are on Water Street.

This is one of the best museum stores in America. Open daily, 10am to 5pm.

OLDE MYSTICK VILLAGE
Rte. 27 and Coogan Blvd., Mystic

This is a cute spot, although it can get crowded. It's a shopping mall but it has been carefully set up as a colonial village—with footpaths leading to the stores, which are all painted in burnished colonial colors.

There's a pond with some geese, and stocks on the village green. The place has got a lovely, meandering feel and is surprisingly noncommercial. But it's still a mall and a major tourist attraction. There's a bank with cash machines, some 60 shops, rest rooms, even an old-fashioned meetinghouse. **Franklin's General Store** is dark, but your eyes will quickly adjust to seek out the souvenirs, gifts, and local food products (including cheeses, fudge, and jelly beans). The kids won't want to leave. All stores are open daily; there are extended hours in the evening during the summer season.

WELCOME TO RHODE ISLAND

. . . .

Rhode Island is the smallest state in the Union and as such can feel like a suburb of Massachusetts. While Rhode Island has plenty of American history to share, it seems more like a destination people enjoy as they are passing through to Boston, or to the Cape.

Providence, the capital city, has some very impressive architecture of both the big-building variety and the little Federal-home variety. It is also the home of Brown University and the Rhode Island School of Design, which means there are a number of talented artists and craftspeople in the area. Providence itself is rather depressed these days; there's more tourist action in Newport.

NEWPORT

. . . .

Although Newport has its reputation as a summer watering hole for old money, you'll have no trouble spending your new money in town at the many stores or nearby factory outlets. Newport is touristy in season, but has enough lovely shopping areas and enough exciting retail for you to realize you've come to a very special place. The crowds that wander by in their shorts and T-shirts (ice-cream cones in hand) would surely make Mrs. Vanderbilt faint—and will certainly amuse you as you contrast the surroundings with the crowd. Nonetheless, the stores range from elegant to funky, and Newport delivers as a destination.

Newport has been around for a long time; its fame and history are not related to the colonial era, but rather the golden age before World War I when money was money and income tax did not exist. Seeing the restored mansions, whether you drive by or actually take one of the tours, is a big part of making the scene. So is appreciating tennis and sailing. The facts that there are some outstanding examples of colonial architecture and that the oldest synagogue in the U.S. is right in town are just two of Newport's many secret appeals.

The Lay of the Land

The main center of Newport lies up against the water. Thames Street (rhymes with James; do not pronounce this in the British manner) is the main shopping and strolling drag. It's a bit difficult to drive along the first time, as it zigs and zags and occasionally changes name; it's much more sensible to walk. In fact, driving in Newport is not particularly easy—and finding a parking space could become a new Olympic sport. Also note that on-street parking after 6pm is reserved for stickered local residents only. Pick your hotel so you have free parking in a location where you can walk to everything. Otherwise, park for the day in one of the many Thames Street lots ($6 to $10 per day) and hike.

Between Thames Street and the water there are several mall strips and little alleys and wharves and docks all filled with beckoning shops. The Brick Market Mall marks the beginning of Thames Street shopping.

The greatest congregation of TTs are in this area. Running parallel above Thames Street is Spring Street, which has some shops as well. They are clustered mostly between Church and Broadway. Above Spring Street is Bellevue Avenue, home to Mansion Row.

There's a second retail area near the Tennis Hall of Fame on Bellevue Avenue; you'll have to move the car to get here.

Antiques shoppers and junkers must get over to Franklin Street, which lies between Thames and Spring in the central part of town. This one block is chock-full of antiques shops in converted houses. Most are not prohibitively fancy and are worth a look (see page 74).

Shops are open as much as possible in season because business is business and tourists are shoppers. Most stores are open from 10am to 9pm weekdays and Saturday, and on Sunday from noon until 5pm.

Finds

DEVONSHIRE
304 Thames St., Newport

While you're taking notes on how to perfect your preppy image, stop here for the gardening chapter. Even if you don't garden, you may find gifts or ideas for entertaining or decorating.

EDNA MAE'S MILLINERY
424 Thames St., Newport

Creative, exciting, funky, and fashionable hats for ladies. Expect to pay $80, but these styles are very special.

EXPLORER'S CLUB
138-140 Spring St., Newport

Goods from all over the world blended together to create a natural preppy-outdoorsy look of English and Australian and American sportswear.

IRISH IMPORTS
Bowen's Wharf, Newport

I normally loathe Irish-import stores. So when I send you to this store, you can believe it's a winner—one of the best stores in Newport; one of the best stores in America perhaps. It would even be a good store in Ireland.

Carrying many of the goods from Cleo's in Dublin, the store sells not only the highest-quality Irish-made ready-to-wear, sweaters, linens, woolens, and accessories, but sells them at the same prices as

PICK YOUR OWN

QUONSET VIEW FARM
895 Middle Rd., Portsmouth

This is about 15 or 20 minutes outside of Newport in Portsmouth. If you have some extra time in town and you want to have a ball—go to the farm, where you can pick your own produce in a scenic field overlooking Narragansett Bay. We swear these were the best strawberries we have ever had in our lives. We paid 85¢ a pound and had a ball. July is blueberry season; in the fall you can get pumpkins.

at Cleo's. These things are not inexpensive, but they are the best in the world.

RUE DE FRANCE
78 Thames St., Newport

One of the most famous mail-order businesses in home decorating, famous for their French cotton-lace country curtains, has a shop at their headquarters right here on Thames Street.

FULL SWING
474 Thames St., Newport

This is a fabric source to the trade only, except in the month of July when the public can scarf it all up.

THE SAIL LOFT
Bowen's Wharf, Newport

This is where men can completely deck themselves out in the proper Newport/New England/"Let's go sailing" look. There's a loft with more merchandise above the main floor.

Chapter Eight

. . . .

BOSTON & THE 'BURBS

WELCOME TO BOSTON

. . . .

Now, what did Mark Twain say were America's best little cities? Weren't they San Francisco, New Orleans, San Antonio, and Boston? Maybe so. And rightly so, since Boston, and its city across the river, Cambridge, offer a whole lot of living (and shopping) for those who visit on vacation or business, for a short time or for the long term.

Boston just may be the most American city in America. Certainly it is a showpiece for visitors from all over the country and the world. There is no other city like it, with its combination of new and old American history. This is a city devoted to architecture and books, both of which you can savor every day—even if you aren't much of a shopper.

Boston, with its surrounding cities, has not only history, but culture. In Boston, you get the idea that what you wear is not nearly as important as what you think. In fact, ideas are commerce here and you'll find that retailing is not the most exciting part of the city, but only a facet of the gem that is Boston.

BOSTON METRO AREA

. . . .

The Boston metro area actually stretches into several states; people commute from as far away as

Maine and Rhode Island. Many a smart traveler has used the Providence airport to get to Boston, Cape Cod, and the area—and, of course, as I mentioned in Chapter 2, airfares are quite competitive in this market (see page 17).

Along with this commuter sprawl, there is also the tourist trail. Some of America's most important historical sites are in the Boston area, so that a trip to Boston often means hopping in the car and heading out of town a few miles to see the place where that shot was "heard round the world." All sorts of places make up the Boston state of mind.

Note that the shopping in downtown Boston is very sophisticated these days, and getting more and more European as each day passes, but as you get to the tourist sites, things get more touristy and more professionally cute—that's not a bad thing, it's just not reality. In between you have a very high profile discount business, in Boston itself and in outlying areas, brimming with factory outlets. Boston is indeed the hub of Yankee thrift.

THE SHOPPING SCENE
. . . .

Boston has changed enormously in the last two years: It's gotten much more sophisticated, much more with it. Dare I say it? After several hundred years as an important American city, Boston is just now emerging as a shopping city!

Sure, you'll still find Boston Brahmins who wear velvet headbands (even in summer), but Boston has a with-it feel that is brand new and quite becoming. And the discount shopping, once relegated to **Filene's Basement** and hope-to-get-lucky bargains, has become very sophisticated as well; The Basement now competes with a new downtown **Loehmann's** and with European designer names in the discount stores as well.

Boston is not yet one of America's best shopping cities; it is merely the hub of New England and the entry point for many Europeans who will scarf up the cute, and the bargains. Locals drive an hour or two to get to the factory outlets (it's an hour to **Howland Place** or **Worcester Common** or even Kittery), or they go to New York—or London—to get high fashion and serious selection. They go to **Faneuil Hall** to smile.

The shopping outlook for the tourist is much brighter, since the tourist isn't usually looking for anything special and has limited time to shop. For the person on the run, or the lazy prowl, there are a lot of nice streets to wander (where the stores are in brownstones, or Federal-style houses, or town houses); there are a number of college campuses; and there's the famous **Faneuil Hall**—built into America's first festival marketplace—and the infamous **Filene's Basement**, where they claim to have invented the bargain. There's quite enough to keep you busy!

And with that snazzy new **Loehmann's**, it's whoa there, Paul Revere! One if by land and two if by off-pricer.

SOUVENIR SHOPPING

As one of America's grandest tourist destinations, Boston has plenty of souvenirs for sale. Aside from traditional city items, the big names in merchandising are the home baseball team, the **Red Sox**, the **Bull & Finch Pub** (the bar where the TV show "Cheers" supposedly takes place), and **Harvard University.**

There are a fair amount of colonial-style souvenirs at various historical sites, and, of course, each museum and landmark has its own gift shop.

There is some lobster merchandise, but you'll find plenty of that in Cape Cod if you're headed that way. You'll find TTs galore, many museum stores (see page 173), and enough kitsch to go around.

My two favorite souvenirs from Boston make fun of the local accent: There are T-shirts and coffee cups from Filene's Basement that say "Filene's Basement: Home of the Bahgain" and "Filene's Basement: Bahgains, Bahgain, Bahgains." Then there are baseball caps that say "Bahston." I think it's funny. So sue me.

THE LAY OF THE LAND

Boston was a major American city before there was a United States of America. Today's downtown reflects its colonial heritage. There is a common green (Boston Common), and the city—meaning downtown—is divided into various neighborhoods, each with its own character.

Boston began as a group of villages and enclaves and kept growing by adding on more villages so that today's Boston metropolitan area stretches almost to Maine in the north; Providence, Rhode Island, to the southwest; and Cape Cod to the south.

Most of the metropolitan area is connected by train. The Massachusetts Bay Transportation Authority (MBTA) subway system is simply called the T, and it connects Boston in a sophisticated web that is far better than metropolitan transportation in most any other American city. As a tourist, all you need to know is that Boston is downtown and Cambridge is across the Charles River.

Perhaps the best way to understand it all is to take a few seconds to look out your hotel window or ascend the **Prudential Tower.** When we stay at the **Sheraton Towers** we use the telescopes mounted in the Club Room; from the upper floors of **Swisshôtel Boston** you can see the weather beacon and much of downtown as well. A quick geography lesson from above will neatly show you where you are and where history took place.

GETTING THERE

Logan Airport is an international airport located practically in downtown Boston. It is the hub of New England for domestic and international travel: More and more international flights use Boston as a gateway city.

Note that the newly expanded T. F. Green Airport in Warwick, Rhode Island (outside Providence), considers itself an alternative to Logan. There are airfare wars to prove it; see page 17.

Cab fare (or ferry fare) to the city from the airport is moderate because you're so close; you can also rent a car at the airport. Although Boston does have excellent public transportation, if you are planning to visit Lexington and Concord, or the Cape, or the outlets, you're going to need a car.

A lot of Northeast traffic into Boston comes by **Amtrak** train, which gives you three stops to choose from. The **Route 128** stop is excellent for people who are staying in this area, but it does not have a car-rental agency at the train station—or even that much of a station—so arrange to be picked up if you're coming in here. If you get off in **Back Bay,** you are right at Copley Square and within a minute of all the big hotel chains and the good malls.

GETTING AROUND

While you will need a car to explore outside of the central core of colonial Boston/Cambridge, you can get to most of the normal in-town tourist attractions rather nicely on public transportation. While you'll hear locals grouse about their least favorite T line (which always seems to be red or orange), mass transportation is better than in most American cities and rivals that in many European cities.

There are four lines, each named after a color (red, green, orange, blue). Your children will adore a ride on the T partly because the trains are often trolleys and they go underground, aboveground, and over ground, sometimes all in the length of one trip. You can get free subway maps at tourist offices, the Prudential Center, or some T stations (not all). Using the T like an expert takes a little practice; the lack of connections from line to line extends outward so that you can easily hitch a new line while you are downtown, but it becomes increasingly difficult to connect between lines even when they are very close together.

There is a Boston Passport tourist pass that allows for either 3 or 7 days of unlimited subway and bus use. There are various local monthly passes depending on your needs. Buy this Passport at the tourist kiosk (aboveground) at Boston Common, at the train stations, at some hotels, or at the airport.

If you don't buy the Passport, try to estimate how many tokens you will need for the day and buy them at one fell swoop in the morning; lines can get grueling, especially in rush hour. Some stations demand tokens or exact change, and you can get frantic.

Aside from the basic subway service, there is train service to the outlying commuting areas. You may have to connect to North or South stations, depending on where you are going.

SLEEPING BOSTON

· ·

 SWISSHÔTEL LAFAYETTE
One Avenue de Lafayette, Boston

This is my secret find, my new discovery, my hot value to pass on to you—wait till you see this hotel and its weekend rates! Located inside a skyscraper (you have to take an elevator up to the lobby) this hotel has stunning views, gorgeous rooms, countless amenities, and is located around the corner from Downtown Crossing, **Filene's Basement,** and **Loehmann's,** too.

With a weekend rate of around $125 and all sorts of promotional deals, trust me, this hotel is the best bargain you will find outside of **The Basement.** Speaking of which, ask at the concierge desk for your coupons for 10% off purchases at Filene's Basement! Call 800/621-9200 or 617/451-2600; fax 617/451-0054.

COPLEY PLAZA HOTEL
138 St. James Ave., Boston

If you love grande dame hotels and want a more Back Bay location, you can't go wrong with this hotel, which is across the street from the mall, a block from Newbury Street, and half a block from the Back Bay train station. The lobby is drop-dead gorgeous and dripping with gold and ornamentation; the rooms are large and shabby-chic comfy. Weekend rate at $145 per room. For reservations, call 800/225-7654 or 617/267-5300; fax 617/247-6681.

OMNI PARKER HOUSE
Tremont and School sts., Boston

Great location, perfect for those with young children—it's within walking distance to Faneuil Hall. I've stayed here over the years on book tours and like the feel of the hotel with its modern, updated antiques so that it feels old, but doesn't look it. This hotel has a wide range of special promotions and deals; ask for a discount coupon for 10% off on your purchases at **Filene's Basement.** There's a sensational crafts store in the front corner of the hotel called **Industrie**—don't miss it. Call 800/ THE OMNI or 617/227-8600 for reservations; fax 617/227-2120.

SHERATON BOSTON HOTEL & TOWERS
39 Dalton St., Boston

SHERATON COMMANDER
16 Garden St., Cambridge

Sheraton is headquartered in Boston and offers two convenient Boston properties, one in the heart of Cambridge. Sheraton is one of our main sources when we are touring the area because one phone call can often make all our reservations.

The flagship hotel is in the heart of Back Bay, one block from a T stop and virtually attached to the **Prudential Center** and **Saks Fifth Avenue.** You are one block from Newbury Street and the best uptown shopping Boston can offer. If you are the parent of a college student (can I even be thinking this?) you are near several schools and will find this a convenient place to hang.

One of the reasons I like this hotel is that it has over 1,000 rooms. That might not strike you as intimate, but when I'm on the road—or grabbing a quick weekend in Boston—I don't want to call around to a million places. This hotel is great and it's got tons of space, so I simply depend on the numbers. And I do splurge for Towers, with all the perks, so that while the property isn't intimate, the club room is, and the experience is just super.

There are several restaurants in the hotel, but the best of all is the free breakfast you get as a Towers guest. If you have the whole family with you, you will save money by paying a little extra for the Towers room and getting the free soft drinks, breakfast, newspapers, and use of the telescope. Investigate various promotions, deals, and family prices (kids up to age 17 stay free). For reservations, call 800/325-3535 or 617/236-2000; fax 617/236-1702.

If you want to be closer to the action in Cambridge, there isn't a better location than the Sheraton Commander. It's a small old-fashioned hotel with a great location and casual manner. The hotel fills up fast so book early. For reservations, call 800/325-3535 or 617/547-4800; fax 617/868-8322.

ELECTRONICALLY YOURS

Web Sites

http://www.boston.com   *Boston Globe* tells all.

http://www.ll.mit.edu/Links/metroboston.html
Links to info about the city from MIT.

http://www.std.com/NE/boston.html   Boston-area
info.

http:www.cuisenet.com   Restaurant guide to U.S.
cities, including Boston.

E-Mail

Modern hotels have business centers that allow you
to log on and check your E-mail; the average cost is
$25 an hour but 15-minute increments are sold. Or
you might want to stop by **Cybersmith,** 36 Church
St., Cambridge. For about $10 you get a card worth
online time and then you check your E-mail, post
mail, surf the net, or just order lunch.

Fax Home

Thrilled there's a fax machine in your hotel room?
You may want to read the fine print. It often costs
$3 to receive a fax and far more than that to send
one! The front desk may be far less expensive.
Watch it!

MORE BOSTON INFO

Boston magazine is published monthly; it covers the
local scene and political issues and lists restaurants
and what's happening around town. There is a "Sales
of the Month" column. Also, check *The Boston
Globe* for advertisements of special sale events at
stores like Filene's Basement.

HOURS

Shopping hours in Boston/Cambridge are a combination of student and tourist needs and Puritan ethics. Most large stores open Sunday at noon; there are some bookstores that are open until late at night during the week. Sunday in Cambridge can be pretty slow for retail, although the Coop (the Harvard bookstore) is open. All major malls and suburban outfitters are open on Sunday afternoons.

SNACK & SHOP

The large student population in Boston insures that shoppers can always get off their feet for a cup of coffee and a quick bite. Especially if that bite is a bagel—Boston has been bitten by bagelmania!

Affordable isn't even the name of the game; it is understood in the basic concept to all participants. The croissant craze is over (although still available everywhere) and the bagel craze has begun. My favorite new chain is **Finagle A Bagel,** but there are over a dozen successful bagel chains and zillions of independents.

BOSTON NEIGHBORHOODS

Faneuil Hall

This is a group of buildings, a marketplace, a tourist attraction, and all the rest, but because it's really a destination unto itself, we're calling it a neighborhood. The real name of the neighborhood is Government Center; that's where you will exit the T. Please note that besides the actual Faneuil Hall Marketplace there is a real neighborhood for retail—just take a look at what **The Limited** hath wrought.

Boston/Cambridge

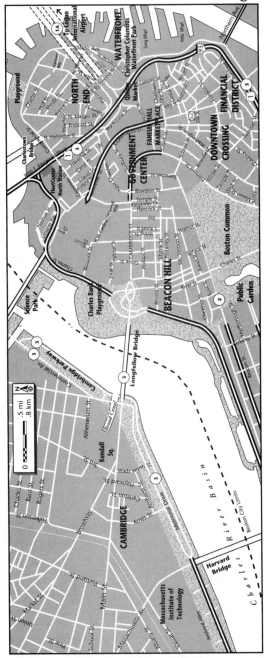

Head straight for **Faneuil Hall,** the one with the grasshopper weathervane. One of the most famous weathervanes in retail history, that grasshopper is the symbol of one of the greatest triumphs in retail. When the three buildings that comprise **Faneuil Hall Marketplace** were just about in the dumpster, the site was rescued and festival shopping was invented. It is the number-one tourist destination in Boston.

Today Faneuil Hall Marketplace consists of three long brick buildings with outdoor alleys between them. **Quincy Market** offers just food. The inside of the buildings and the alleys have all been converted to shops and cafes so you can shop and eat, shop and eat, and then shop and eat some more. Many retailers operate out of pushcarts; there is an open-air flower market. There have been outdoor flea markets.

Retail space is divided between the big-name chains and a handful of stores that have some regional rep—the small guys who are known in Boston and Nantucket or elsewhere nearby but whom you may not have heard of. It's this blend that makes the magic. You can buy T-shirts, souvenirs, rubber stamps, "Cheers" merchandise, and other goodies from kiosks and pushcarts.

If Faneuil Hall weren't enough of a masterpiece, **The Limited** decided to hire a big-name architectural firm (Graham Gund) to build a neoclassical monument to excess as its flagship store. Park your kids at **The Nature Company** (around the corner) and dash in to take in the seven stories of Limited resources (which aren't at all limited): One floor has men's clothing, one floor is **Express,** another sells **Cacique** (an underwear line), and there's even **Limited Too,** a kids' floor. If you are from Europe and aren't familiar with The Limited, now is your time to merge fashion and value and marvel at the combination.

At the opposite end of Faneuil Hall, there's **Marketplace Center,** which is really just a strip center in a good location. Marketplace Center tenants include

The Body Shop, Bath & Body Works, which is the copy of The Body Shop that Limited Express started (but couldn't fit into their big building down the street), as well as several big chains like **Brookstone** and **Banana Republic.**

This entire retail neighborhood is almost always jumping, seven days a week and into the evenings in summer, and on weekends. Most stores open at 10am and close around 9pm. Sunday hours are from noon to 6pm.

North End

The Old North Church is located in the North End; those tourists following The Freedom Trail—a red line painted on the sidewalk that takes you to some very patriotic sights—will find themselves walking under the freeway after they leave Faneuil Hall and traveling a few blocks through the city's Italian neighborhood to reach the church.

I am forced to admit that we got so lost in this web of streets on the other side of the freeway that we had to walk back to Faneuil Hall, hail a taxi, and get a tour of the North End before getting out at the church and starting over. Don't ask me how Paul Revere (or Richard Dawes or whomever) even managed it all.

Once you arrive at the church you can go immediately to their gift shop, which is packed with fun stuff like wool tricornered hats (about $20), blue-and-white transfer plates, pewter this and that, tea towels, refrigerator magnets (a steal at $1), colonial-style candles, and even fake colonial money. There are dolls in colonial dress; there's even the Declaration of Independence for only $1. You'd have to go to a flea market to get a more valuable one. Everyone in the family is going to love this gift shop. The North End neighborhood is 443 acres of historical slum dating back to the early 1600s that is now dotted with Italian restaurants, some Italian food markets, and a few shops for locals and even tourists. People come here at night to eat and during the day to get a sense of history. If you like street markets, come Friday or Saturday morning for the **Haymarket Square** fruit-and-vegetable market.

If Old North Church is your first stop, get off at the Haymarket stop on the T. Visit the church and gift shop and stroll through Paul Revere Mall, which will bring you to Hanover Street, the main drag.

Downtown Crossing

A lot has been done to Downtown Crossing, and while it's not quite charming, it is hopping. To get here use the Park Street or Downtown Crossing stops on the T. Downtown Crossing has to be on your list of Boston landmarks if only because it is home to **Filene's Basement** (see page 168). Now **Loehmann's** has come to Downtown Crossing and several stores have spruced up their act and gotten it together. Even **The Gap** has an outlet store here now at 425 Washington St. **Tello** has reopened next door, for cheap teen clothes.

Copley Place/Prudential Center

Since there are a few neighborhoods in the tony Back Bay shopping area, we are breaking them down very specifically. Copley Place and the Prudential Center are virtually across the street from one another; within these two trade areas you have more upscale shopping and fancy department stores than you can afford to shop in any one day. Others will refer to this part of town simply as Back Bay.

The stores in this area are found in the Prudential Center, in Copley Place (it's a mall, among other things), and in hotels that are part of the two. There are also freestanding stores like **Lord & Taylor.**

Wedged between the Marriott and the Westin hotels is a three-level shopping mall with some of the country's most upscale retailers. Tenants include: **Eileen Fisher, Tiffany & Company, Victoria's**

Secret, Mondi, Ports, North Beach Leather, Brookstone, Caswell Massey, Polo, Rizzoli, Gucci, Louis Vuitton, Williams-Sonoma, etc.

Of special interest is **Coach For Business** because there are only a few of these dotted around America. It's a division of the Coach business, which sells briefcases, ties, gloves, and business-oriented leather goods.

Also note the **Cheers** kiosk, which sells merchandise with the logo of the famous TV bar; **Destination Boston,** with great T-shirts and souvenirs; and **Off Campus** for college sweats and Ts. **Eastern Newsstand** has a great selection of magazines and newspapers from around the world.

There's an **Armani Exchange (A/X),** where jeans cost less than $100, as does most of the merchandise. This one is owned by Saks and has become a major tourist attraction, especially for the international set. (The real Armani is on Newbury Street.)

Inside the hotel lobby there are still more stores, including **W. H. Smith** and **New England Sampler,** a store for regional foodstuffs and gifts, as well as a crafts store, an antiques store, and more.

The Copley Plaza hotels and shops connect by a glass bridge to the Prudential Center and **Saks Fifth Avenue. Lord & Taylor** stands to the side of Saks with its back on Boylston street. By walking through Lord & Taylor, you can easily continue your shopping spree on Boylston Street.

To get there, take the Copley T stop, or it's an easy walk from the Prudential or Hynes Convention Center/Auditorium T stops.

Boylston Street

This downtown street runs parallel with Newbury Street and is not the main retailing drag. Because of its location, immediately between Prudential Center and Newbury Street, there is some retail built mostly to serve the working population in the nearby office towers. And here and there, like wildflowers, are some very special buildings for shoppers with money and taste. Check out **Heritage On The Park** (at Arlington and Boylston streets), a mixed-use building for classy stores and eats, including a Sonia Rykiel store and a branch of Hermès.

Don't miss **Brodney** (811 Boylston St.), which is a fancy antiques store with great treasures stacked high and buried deep. They have antique jewelry as well as dishes, paintings, and furniture. The other diamond in the Boylston Street crown is a spiffy new building called **500** at—you guessed it—500 Boylston St. This is one of those sparkling, multi-use complexes that are all the rage; its lower levels are devoted to, get this, **Marshall's,** the off-price store!

Talbot's and **Eddie Bauer** are here as well. There's a **Hard Rock Cafe** here; stock up at their store on the Ts and sweats, considered high fashion by teens.

To explore Boylston, take the T to either Hynes Convention Center/Auditorium or Arlington. (The stops are at opposite ends of Boylston Street.)

Newbury Street

The core of Boston's retail scene is Newbury Street, where the chic and the sleek meet to shop and stare. Although locals would like you to think this is Boston's answer to Rodeo Drive, or even the Faubourg St. Honore—it's, well, much more American.

I say that Newbury Street has no twin because it is both funky and elegant, a rare combination that wins me over every time. Also, they haven't built a Disney Store, a Levi's Store, or a Niketown yet, so you can still enjoy the architecture and just wander and even window-shop.

About half the stores are local, small-time retailers just trying to get by, pay the rent, and offer you some decent shopping; the other half are the serious players, the giant money men you see in any other big city or fancy mall. You come to Newbury Street, then, not specifically for certain shops, but for the ambience, the adventure, the sheer fun of it. Strolling down the street, taking in the architecture and the trees, is as much a part of the experience as anything else.

The street is more fancy at the Arlington end, more funky (and studenty) at the Mass Avenue end. Pick your poison, but do walk the length of it at least one way if not both ways.

Wear comfortable shoes, arrive at the Hynes Convention Center/Auditorium T stop and begin at the huge **Tower Records.** Even if you don't want any music, you might want to peek inside and take a look at the crowd and the design of the building. Welcome to the 1990s; welcome to the Boston of students and alternative culture.

And speaking of students, if yours has arrived at school without many of the comforts of home (Aaron forgot his pillow), there's a **Bed, Bath & Beyond** right on Newbury Street, across from Tower Records. The store is on a lower level so there's only a small entry door at the street. Everything you need for dorm or apartment or first home is here, and discounted.

Stroll along Newbury Street to the Ritz-Carlton Hotel. Stop and shop as much as your wallet permits. Don't miss **Urban Outfitters** (no. 361), where nostalgia for the late 1960s is so overwhelming you'll either laugh or cry (if you're over 40 anyway). This is where teens and preteens go crazy for inexpensive imports and clothes and tote bags with daisies on them. **Reebok** (no. 344) was the first concept store and the beginning of something big (see page 158). **Patagonia** (no. 346) is the place for colorful, outdoorsy sporty clothes.

Nomad (no. 279) is actually one of my favorite stores in the world, even though they carry mostly imports of ethnic clothes and handcrafts that seem to work better in the Boston/Cambridge milieu than anywhere else. They have a lot of Mexican things that touch my soul, and the people that own the store, or organize the displays, seem to be made of the right stuff. Even if you don't buy this kind of stuff, stop by and enjoy.

Betsey Johnson, Banana Republic, and **The Nature Company** are all in their own little mini-mall of a converted redbrick schoolhouse, followed almost immediately by **Cignal,** a mass retailer successfully selling cutting-edge fashion that is always hot, and **The Gap** (no. 201) where all of America dresses.

By now you are crossing Exeter Street and have got to get a look—from the outside—at the building that houses **Waterstone's,** the British booksellers (no. 26 Exeter St.). It used to be a movie theater and the rehab is terrific. And yes, books cost less in the U.S. than in Britain. Once inside, you almost expect to be handed a bag of popcorn as you walk through the levels of green carpet and books, books, books.

Back on Newbury, you've got **The Society of Arts and Crafts** (no. 175); **La Ruche** (no. 174) for household gifts, tabletop, painted birdhouses, and the cluttered look of Victorian whimsy; **Agnes B.** (no. 172), the avant-garde women's ready-to-wear line; and **W. D. & Co.** (no. 165) for very arty clothing and accessories, mostly for women, but there is some menswear and the Czech & Speake line of toiletries from London's Jermyn Street.

Anokhi (no. 156), is an international chain that doesn't have that many branches in the U.S. and may be new to you. The look is slightly ethnic and ethereal with fabrics from the Far East. **Rodier** (no. 144) and **Country Road** (no. 140) are branches of the well-known French and Australian concerns; Rodier specializes in knits (great for travel); Country Road has weekend looks for men and women. **Joseph A. Banks,** who practically defines preppy for men and women, has just moved to 399 Boylston Street. For those same customers, there's also the **Junior League Bargain Box** (no. 117), a thrift shop— of course.

Continue on to **Pierre Deux** (no. 111) in a town house with a few levels of Les Olivades fabrics and French-country looks we adore.

You're reaching the higher-end real estate now and will spot **Jacadi** (no. 110) for the kiddies, **Laura Ashley** (no. 83), **The Coach Store** (no. 75), and **Timberland** (no. 71). You are now ready to face **Louis** (no. 234 Berkeley), the king of upscale retail in Boston. See page 157 for the lowdown. Whatever you do, don't miss this monument to money and refined good taste.

As you move along the final blocks before the park and the Ritz-Carlton Hotel, you'll see the old standards like **Brooks Brothers** (no. 46), which invented the preppy look and now even sells it to the British at Marks & Spencer stores in London (M&S owns BB). Also nearby are **Cartier** (no. 38), **Guy Laroche** (no. 32), and **Joseph Abboud** (no. 37). Abboud got his start at Louis and had the chutzpah to open his own multilevel, mostly beige, classy temple to elegant men's and women's clothing for the wealthy. There's also **Ann Taylor** (no. 18) for mortal women who need an office look, and **Burberrys** (no. 2), the British classic.

Since you've now reached a dead end, you can either fade into the Ritz-Carlton for tea, or turn right on Arlington Street and walk one block to Boylston Street. Or head for the swan boats in the park.

To get to Newbury Street, take the Green line to Hynes Convention Center/Auditorium.

Beacon Hill

It's so very old Boston, old money. While you might not be able to move into the little redbrick Federal houses that line the streets and work their way up the hills, you can stroll the shopping street and soak up the atmosphere and charm of another time. Charles Street has a wonderful neighborhood feeling to it, so that along with the old-fashioned colonial air, you get a sense of what must be the true Boston. There's a number of antiques shops (many without names on the front, just a sign that says ANTIQUES) and a few neighborhood businesses.

You'll enjoy **Period Furniture Hardware Company** (no. 123) with lanterns as well as taps, knockers, and other brass hardware for a house restoration or renovation. Our favorite item is the old-fashioned glass window panes ($80 each). **George Gravert Antiques** (no. 122), **Antique Danish Country** (no. 138), **Marika's Antiques** (no. 132), **Antique Ireland** (no. 103), and **Finders Keepers** (no. 93) are all great little shops to browse for antiques, china, and knickknacks. **Grossman Antiques** (no. 51) is another good choice, and then there's the **Beacon Hill Thrift Shop** (no. 15) where we saw a set of needlepoint dinner-chair cushions that I still wish we had bought.

To get there, take the Red line to the Charles Street stop.

Harvard Square

I keep a watercolor of Harvard Square (on a postcard by Linda Levine) taped to the wall next to my desk to remind me of all the mystery and fantasy of Harvard Square. The postcard is a beauty. The reality of shopping in the Harvard Square area of Cambridge is something else indeed. In the heyday of Design/Research, when we were young, we thought Harvard Square was a really neat place. Now we aren't too impressed. But we have found a shopping district we adore just down the street.

There are some good things for shoppers in the Harvard Square area, but they are not fashionable, except maybe the **Origins** store, which was Estee Lauder's first. **The Harvard Coop** (see page 157) is one of the best bookstores in the world. The newsstand next to the T station is fabulous and worthy of hours of your time and most of your spending money. The rest of the shopping is grouped around Brattle Street and, despite a new building meant to jazz up the area with an **HMV** record store and some branch retail like **The Gap, Ann Taylor,** and **Crate & Barrel,** it's pretty stale.

To get there, take the Red line to the Harvard Square stop.

Local Heroes

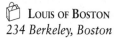 HARVARD COOP
1400 Massachusetts Ave., Cambridge

Going way back to the late 1800s, the Coop has been *the* place to shop for both Harvard-Wellesley students and pretenders alike. There are two buildings. One sells dry goods, rather like a general store—clothing, underwear, pantyhose, and merchandise covered with college logos. To get your books you cross the street out the back end of the dry-goods store, or you take the bridge on the third floor to find yourself in one of the best bookstores in the world. There are even rest rooms here.

 APRIL CORNELL
Faneuil Hall, N. Market, Boston

You may know this business as Handblock; it has been going by the designer's name only for a few years. I also rave about this chain in everything I write; I am their biggest fan. For the uninitiated, Ms. Cornell does sort of a country-French look with great colors on Indian fabrics—she sells home design, clothes for women and children, and some tabletop that's very country rustic (like pottery and gift items). While there are a handful of stores all over America, the one at Faneuil Hall also serves as an outlet and has great sales as well as bargain baskets filled with cast-offs that can cost as little as $3 per item. You get a pillowcase for $3, not a tablecloth.

 LOUIS OF BOSTON
234 Berkeley, Boston

I cannot adequately describe Louis of Boston because it is a store you just have to feel. It feels like old money and splendor, and refined elegance and taste. The store is in a restored mansion and is simply gorgeous. Even if you aren't much of a shopper, this should be on your list of Boston landmarks. The style is more European than preppy; they do have sales. Men's and women's clothing. Don't bring the kids. Note that a few years ago a cafe was added on, and that cafe has now moved into the fame and fortune list of must-dos with awards and kudos going to the chef. This entire experience—shopping and eating—is simply the essence of sophistication in Boston.

REEBOK
344 Newbury St., Boston

REEBOK WAREHOUSE STORE
300 Technology Centre Dr., Stoughton

With their factory in a Boston suburb, and a handful of outlet stores all over New England, Reebok's move into regular retail with a glitzy store on Newbury Street has further endeared them to tourists and locals alike. Even though Niketown moved in down the block with their showbiz, high fashion, high-tech whiz-bang approach to selling, Reebok is the local brand.

The store is not Niketown, but that's probably the point. It offers 5,000 square feet of clothing, shoes, and bold ideas still in the test stages, so that some of the merchandise sold here is not available anywhere else. More importantly, at least to your kids, is they do have The Pump Room, which is an area of the store devoted to the various styles of The Pump.

A percentage of the profits are donated to different socially responsible organizations. And yes, we're glad you noticed—the entire ceiling is waffled like an athletic shoe. If you are from England, you might want to go to the factory store in Stoughton just so you can return with stories of low prices for "train-ers." Friends at home won't believe it. Note that only at the Reebok-owned stores can you get all 20 colors in the Reebok Freestyle range.

SHREVE, CRUMP & LOW
330 Boylston St., Boston

Since 1800 this has been the place for bridal regis-try; the appropriate place from which to send not only wedding gifts, but special-occasion, baby, and house gifts. Not only does it tell the recipient that you want to send them the very best, it shows your great respect for Boston tradition. Formal, fancy, and not-so-traditional silver, crystal, and dishes from a store that also has the reputation of being the best jeweler in town. They are famous for their estate and antique pieces.

BREAD & CIRCUS
115 Prospect St., Cambridge

This is one of about a half dozen branch stores of the most famous health-food store in the area; they even have a store in Providence. This store is a local legend when it comes to local produce, offering fresh as well as prepared foods.

BASIC BOSTON RESOURCES FROM A TO Z
. . . .
Antiques

The Boston antiques scene is actually multilayered with stores in town and in assorted suburbs in almost every direction. The most fun any lover of antiques and antiques shops will have on a day in the city is the prowl up and down **Charles Street.** Some of the side streets also have worthwhile offer-ings, such as **Gallagher Christopher Antiques** at 84 Chestnut St.

Metro Area Antiques Centers

Boston Antiques Center, 54 Canal St., Boston, MA   Open Tuesday through Saturday, 10am to 5:30pm; Sunday, noon to 5pm; closed Monday.

Massachusetts Antiques Coop, 100 Felton St., Waltham, MA   Open Wednesday through Monday, 10am to 5pm; Thursday until 8pm. Closed Tuesday.

Cambridge Antique Market, 201 Msgr. O'Brien Hwy., Cambridge, MA   Open Tuesday through Sunday, 11am to 6pm.

Camden Companies Inc., is a huge antiques and decorative-arts store at 211 Berkeley St. in Back Bay.

There are antiques centers in both Boston and Cambridge; there is a small antiques department at the **Women's Educational & Industrial Union,** 356 Boylston—I wasn't knocked out, but you'll pass by here in your everyday exploration, and it's fun. If you're looking for a day trip, check out Salem and Essex. Essex has the largest concentration of antiques shops in the area.

Auctions

Check out the Auction section of the **Sunday** *Boston Globe* for a page of tiny print and tons of auction—and antiques—listings.

Beauty

 FRESH
121 Newbury St., Boston

One of those incredible Euro drugstores that makes you want to buy everything even though the prices are ridiculous. Suddenly a $10 soap seems worth the money. Assorted international brands.

30 NEWBURY
30 Newbury St., Boston

Day spa of the moment with treatments as well as aromatherapy treatments and products.

CONDOM WORLD
332 Newbury St., Boston

Downstairs from the comics store; something for everyone. Point it out to your college students.

Beer

Boston is home to a zillion microbreweries; you can drink your way through the city and the 'burbs. Mix your own signature brew at **The Modern Brewer,** 99 Dover St. in Sommerville (☎ 800/ SEND-ALE or 617/629-0400).

Books

Boston is the place where Hester Prynne received her Scarlet *A,* Emerson penned his essay on "Self-Reliance," and Longfellow made a folk hero out of Paul Revere (although William Dawes actually swung the signaling lantern from Old North Church).

A century and a half later, Louisa May Alcott, Henry David Thoreau, and the members of the Thanatopsis Society are history, but Boston's literary tradition continues with the likes of Robert Lowell, E. B. White, Robert McCloskey, Adrienne Rich, and George Higgins. Boston can still boast of active trade-book publishers such as Houghton Mifflin, Addison-Wesley, and Little, Brown, as well as *Atlantic Monthly,* the nation's longest-running literary magazine, founded in 1857. It is also home to a great public library, as well as several well-stocked private ones, and it remains one of America's (and the world's) best book cities for both new and used books.

AVENUE VICTOR HUGO BOOKSHOP
339 Newbury St., Boston

This is a tribute to a Parisian bibliotheque. The shop has a fairly large selection of used books as well as new books, cards, comics, and magazines. We found the business section to be particularly well stocked with company histories, management primers, and investment advice. Although the sports section is small, we were able to locate a book on the Red Sox we had admired but hadn't found for several years. What the store lacks in size is more than made up in the service department. Open Monday to Friday, 9am to 9pm; Saturday, 10am to 8pm; and Sunday, noon to 8pm.

BOSTON ATHENAEUM
10^1/$_2$ Beacon St., Boston

Any serious book lover begins his or her tour here in an oasis of solitude. The Athenaeum, founded in 1807, is a private library open to members and researchers by prior appointment. Along with a staggering collection of books about Boston and a copy of nearly every work by a Boston author, you'll also find a part of George Washington's library. The Athenaeum also sells postcards and the like. On Wednesdays, the Athenaeum serves tea, the perfect time to glimpse a world in which the fictional George Apley would have felt right at home.

THE BRATTLE BOOK SHOP
9 West St., Boston

The Brattle is a secondhand bookshop with tons of stock on Boston, American History, and the Military. Everything is well organized on two floors, and prices are modest enough even for a New

Englander to appreciate. The shop also features *Life* magazines from the 1950s and 1960s for $2 a copy.

GOODSPEED'S BOOK SHOP
7 Beacon St., Boston (maps, genealogy, prints)
2 Milk St., Boston (used books)

Just across the street from the Athenaeum, their motto is "Anything that's a book." The motto befits a family firm that began selling books in Boston 3 years before the Red Sox were founded. Goodspeed is not the New England equivalent of "Howdy, pardner," but rather, the name of the family that's been running the shop since 1898. (The current owner is George Goodspeed.) As much a Boston institution as the Marathon, Goodspeed's heritage is proud enough to warrant a book, *Yankee Bookseller,* published by Houghton Mifflin.

Goodspeed's has an abundance of material devoted to genealogy. In addition to such books as *Mayflower Marriages* and *In Search of Your Canadian Roots,* the shop has more than 2,000 volumes devoted to descendants of specific families—Cabots, Lowells, and Lodges as well as DiLorenzos, McSweeneys, and Rosenzweigs. Goodspeed's offers catalogs of its offerings, and lists everyone from the Abbeys to the Youngs, along with local histories from Alabama to Wisconsin.

In addition to the genealogy books, you'll also find other kinds of Americana. The Beacon Street shop has a wide selection of prints, maps, and autographs, as well as books. A recent catalog offered original prints by John James Audubon. (The *Carolina Turtle Dove* print was offered at $11,500.)

If this original store doesn't have what you're looking for, walk over to Milk Street, near the Old Meeting House, and check out a second location. This store is given over entirely to secondhand books. While there are first editions and books of hand-colored botanical and ornithological illustrations, we particularly liked the wide selection of Heritage Press books.

THE GLOBE CORNER BOOK STORE
1 School St., Boston
500 Boylston St., Boston
28 Church St., Harvard Sq., Cambridge

At the corner of Washington and School streets you'll find this modern establishment with a history as rich as Goodspeed's. Originally the home of Anne Hutchinson, who came to Boston in 1634, the present building was completed in 1718 and became a bookstore in 1829. A bit later, William Ticknor and James Fields took the place over and made it the single most important literary address in America.

The booksellers turned publishers by issuing Longfellow's epic poem *Evangeline*. Later, the partners published Emerson, Hawthorne, Thoreau, and Longfellow; became the American publishers for Thackeray and Tennyson; and became part of Houghton Mifflin. Like its sister store in Cambridge, the Globe is chock-full of books on travel, along with globes, maps, and atlases. This shop also devotes space to children's books, and even publishes a newsletter devoted to the subject called *The Scoop*.

They have a terrific travel shop on Boylston Street, a great, cozy, wonderfully university-ish branch off Harvard Square, and yet another branch in North Conway, New Hampshire (Settler's Green, Route 16). They even have a toll-free ordering number (☎ 800/358-6013) and issue "Frequent Traveller Cards," which entitle customers to a 25% discount on a gift purchase after they've spent $60 at the Globe. Prices are considered to be lower than at the Harvard Coop.

TRIDENT BOOKSELLERS & CAFE
338 Newbury St., Boston

A combination bookstore and coffee shop that bills itself as "Boston's Alternative." If you've absent-mindedly left your Tarot cards home (hey, these things happen) or feel an overwhelming urge to throw the I Ching, you'll find a wide variety of New Age paraphernalia here along with books on women's studies, nutrition, ecology, politics, and astrological matters. The food side is devoted to salads, quiches, and desserts.

HARVARD COOP
1400 Massachusetts Ave., Cambridge

Part bookstore, park general store, part souvenir store, part icon and landmark, the Coop (as in chicken; one syllable not two!) sells every book in the world. You can spend years here. The major gossip is that the venerable icon has gone into business with Barnes & Noble, America's leading discount chain, to beef up stock and get modern and hip. They expect to expand in their college selection as well. Don't fret that Barnes & Noble will ruin the charm; they already run college bookstores for several area universities, and no one is complaining. Boola Boola.

Brides

FILENE'S BASEMENT BRIDAL SALE
246 Washington St., Boston

This extravaganza is famous in Boston lore and worth the trip for any prospective bride with gumption. Entire wedding parties show up at this event where they fight for—and over—the samples. Women who are size 20 insist they are a size 8. Mothers of the bride vie for the best pink pleated gowns of the season. Our friend Mary survived the sale and explains the basic strategy: "You've got to have something to trade." You push your way onto the scene and grab as many dresses as you can; you then trade them with the other brides until you find one you like. Savings are so sublime that it's all worth the aggravation. Watch for the announcement of the sale or call 617/542-2011 for more information.

Zazou
80 Winchester St., Newton

This is a tiny resale shop in Newton (not far from Boston) that has absolutely gorgeous wedding gowns at rather reasonable prices. If you want specific directions, call 617/527-2555. Believe me, this was one of the most special stores of this type I've ever seen, so it's worth calling them, asking about size selection, and driving over for a look.

Priscilla of Boston
137 Newbury St., Boston

The single-most famous name in specialty wedding gowns in America. Located upstairs on the second floor. The choice of many famous (and White House) brides.

Michelle Kelly
Call for appointment and address:
☎ *617/232-8040*

Custom-made gowns from a resource I found in the *Boston Globe*. Michelle Kelly creates for a label called Willows & Ivy but also does custom work, which does take about three months, so no shotgun brides, please. Simple elegance before Carolyn Bessette Kennedy made it the vogue.

Department & Specialty Stores

Bloomingdale's
Rte. 9, Chestnut Hill

Those who are driving along Route 9 need our warning right now: There are two Bloomingdale's located in the Chestnut Hill area. The Bloomie's in the Chestnut Hill Mall is strictly a furniture and home-furnishings store. If you want clothes, stop at the small branch store in a strip mall on Route 9, one block before the mall.

FILENE'S
426 Washington St., Boston

Now that I've taught you the difference between Filene's and Filene's Basement, let's take a look at this big-name Boston department store. This is an old venerated name in retailing with a steady stock of department-store goods and a mix of fashion names. The emphasis is on family and fashion; that means the store is a little stodgy compared to Macy's, which is across the street.

MACY'S
450 Washington St., Boston

Whoa, here's the new kid on the block—Jordan Marsh is now Macy's! The store has concentrated on a youthful approach with an emphasis on contemporary looks for the whole family. The push is for a modern, young image. Many branch stores.

NEIMAN MARCUS
Copley Place, Boston

The leading purveyor of fashion with an edge, Neiman Marcus is known to be a little more expensive than the competition, so it's not the place for bargain hunters. This branch store is very carefully stocked to feature unique and unusual items in order to prevent locals from shopping in New York or London.

SAKS FIFTH AVENUE
Prudential Plaza, Boston

OK, so we know you probably have a Saks in your hometown or have been to the flagship store on Fifth Avenue and cannot imagine why we are sending you to a branch store. Well, here's why: Branch stores in different cities are merchandised differently and this branch of Saks puts their trust in fashion names.

There is a small Chanel boutique (there isn't even one in the New York Fifth Avenue store). They also have programs for out-of-towners, international guests, conventioneers, etc.

Discount Stores & Off-Pricers

FILENE'S BASEMENT
426 Washington St., Boston

Filene's Basement is indeed located in the basement—two levels of subterranean space beneath Filene's department store. Filene's is a perfectly respectable department store; Filene's Basement is owned by a completely different company that has nothing to do with Filene's—except share its foundation.

A million years ago, when there were no factory outlets and discount was a whispered word, Filene's Basement functioned as the dumping ground for this country's leading retailers. If Neiman Marcus couldn't sell it, out it went—off to Filene's Basement for sale at a pitifully low price, complete with label, hangtags, and original price ticket. All the major specialty stores, as well as designer boutiques, dumped their unsold goods at Filene's Basement and the shopping was great. Note the use of the past tense.

With the advent of the factory outlet, Filene's Basement has changed dramatically. Also note that a number of years ago Filene's Basement went national, so there are now 50 stores in a handful of states. What you have is sort of an all-in-one outlet store where prices and selection are best on merchandise that comes from stores that don't have nearby outlets. I've seen Ferragamo shoes for $88 a pair! Brooks Brothers trousers for $14 a pair! And these finds were at branch stores.

But wait! That's not the end of the story. There are two more ingredients that make the original Filene's Basement a bonanza: an automatic markdown policy (only available in the downtown Boston store) and what they call "retail stock."

Reduced Confessions

So I was shopping in **The Basement** one day and, in the men's department, in a bin, I found the Ferragamo sweater of my dreams. It had no price tag on it. I hunted all over and finally, inside the pocket, I found a package of half-eaten bubble gum and a price tag for $185. The date on the back showed that in two days the item would go to half-price. I could have hidden the sweater in a corner and come back in two days.

But I didn't want to have to change my schedule and I wanted it then. So I took it to a cashier and explained there was no tag, hoping that things would go my way. Instead, they made me wait about 20 minutes and then tagged the sweater at $199. I thought I would die. I didn't dare tell them about the gum and the tag in the pocket so I asked the policy, explaining that similar sweaters in the same bin were $185 and had been there a long time.

It was explained to me that the house policy decrees that when a garment has no tag, it's given a new tag and dated all over again from that day forward!

Even if you've been to a branch of Filene's Basement, you owe yourself this treat, but don't bring the kids, the husband, or the mother-in-law—unless you're talking about the bridal sale (see page 165), when future mothers-in-law are expected to do their share. This is not a shopping experience for the faint-hearted; Filene's Basement is the second-biggest tourist draw in Boston, and 10,000 to 20,000 people shop their way through each day. Just do it. And if you don't like it, get out quickly before you lose your sanity.

Do make it your business when you are in town to look in the *Boston Globe* early each morning, as the sales and specials are always announced there.

Very often the main store will open at 8am for a big event. Sometimes people even stand in line overnight or line up at 6am. Also check the paper for discount coupons, which might be printed right into the advert; these entitle you to 15% (or whatever) off a purchase.

Ask your hotel if they have discount coupons, as several of the city's best hotels are in a hospitality plan with Filene's Basement and will give you a discount coupon just for the asking.

In order to keep its edge over Loehmann's, The Basement has opened an area they call **The Vault,** which is stocked with handpicked merchandise from Europe's biggest designers. I bought two Ferragamo handbags: a leather, killer, drop-dead bag for $299 and a tiny satin evening bag for $129.

LOEHMANN'S
Jeweler's Bldg., Washington St., Boston

While Loehmann's has been in the metro area for years, this entry into downtown and into Filene's Basement's backyard is not only a declaration of war with The Basement but a declaration of the new Loehmann's, a company that has recently taken a very big stand in big-city retail. Their stores in Manhattan and Boston are in key traffic areas and for the first time show that the off-pricer is not afraid of department stores any more.

The store sells mostly women's clothing but there are some men's furnishings (underwear, robes, socks), shoes, and intimate apparel. There are plus sizes as well as petite sizes. Frankly, there's some of everything.

European Big Names

GIORGIO ARMANI
22 Newbury St., Boston

BURBERRYS
2 Newbury St., Boston

Escada
Heritage on the Garden, 280 Boylston St., Boston

Hermès
Heritage on the Garden, 280 Boylston St., Boston

MCM
4/6 Newbury St., Boston

Next
306 Newbury St., Boston

Rodier
144 Newbury St., Boston

Sonia Rykiel
Heritage on the Garden, 280 Boylston St., Boston

Gianni Versace
12 Newbury St., Boston

Home Style

April Cornell
Faneuil Hall, N. Marketplace, Boston

While she sells more than *objets* for the home, this is the heart of my home style and I buy many table and bed linens here. I drive to Boston just for the sales. The goods are made in India but have a Provençal quality to them.

Domain
7 Newbury St., Boston

Domain Warehouse
51 Morgan St., Norwood

A unique store in the home-design field and a local hero to boot. The furniture and style are many steps above Pottery Barn and low-end Americana, yet they are affordable and slightly mass market. You get a big bang for your buck; lots of big comfy chairs and sofas and high-end looks. Especially fun during a sale period. Some gift items.

Should you love the style but find the prices a tad too high and don't want to wait for a seasonal sale, you might want to find your way to the warehouse, where damages and old models are sold at roughly half price. This means that things often cost just under $1,000 instead of $1,500—so I am not talking giveaway prices here.

Note: The warehouse is only open for the "long weekend"—Thursday through Saturday 10am to 5pm; Sunday, noon to 5pm. They will do an area delivery, for a fee.

Second note: Once you've made it to Norwood, there is another furniture outlet a block away, **In Warehouse Store,** at 77 Carnegie Row.

PIERRE DEUX
111 Newbury St., Boston

Even though they are phasing out their Soleiado collection and selling more and more things from Les Olivades, this store still has a stunning collection of fabrics, home furnishings, and charm.

Malls

Boston and the outlying suburbs are packed with a variety of large- and small-sized malls. If you're driving into the outlying areas and want to check out a big complex, you'll usually find all the standards: big department stores like **Neiman Marcus, Saks,** and **Bloomingdale's;** chain stores like **Brooks Brothers, Laura Ashley,** and **Benetton.**

The ritziest malls are the **Chestnut Hill Mall,** 199 Boylston St., Chestnut Hill, and **The Atrium,** 300 Boylston St., Chestnut Hill. As you can tell from the address, they are virtually across the street from each other. However, you're in suburbia now so this is not walking distance, and if you are driving, it's a tad tricky to get off the road and cut back properly for The Atrium. But I know you're clever and you can figure it out. On the other hand, I'm sure you've seen malls before, and you are more interested in gravestone rubbing.

If you are needing a mall for sheer convenience because you're in town for a parent weekend or you are loading up, the **Cambridge Galleria** is large (100 stores), spacious, and easy to shop. It even has a **J. Crew** store. There's a free shuttle bus from the Kendall Stop (Red Line); this feels like it's in the middle of nowhere, but it's really easy to do.

Museum Shops

BOSTON MUSEUM OF FINE ARTS
465 Huntington Ave., Boston
Faneuil Hall, Boston

Tell the guard you just want to shop in the Museum Store, and he probably won't make you buy a ticket to the museum. The shop is located in an oval space behind glass walls and offers a wide range of goods. If you've used the catalog—which is great—you might be a bit disappointed in the selection at the store.

The museum, like the Met in New York, also has freestanding museum shops in shopping areas not related to the museum itself. There's one at Faneuil Hall that's convenient enough.

Meanwhile, watch the paper for ads for warehouse sales, usually held in spring and fall over a weekend at the distribution center in Avon, Massachusetts. Call 508/584-5505 for dates, details, or directions.

HARVARD UNIVERSITY MUSEUM OF NATURAL HISTORY
24 Oxford St., Cambridge

There are four connected museums here; gift shops sell dinosaur goodies that are always popular with the kids.

ISABELLA STEWART GARDNER MUSEUM
The Fenway at Palace Rd., Boston

The city's most extravagant museum for those interested in decorative arts. The gift shop is very special and offers reproduction designs from the collection, as well as the usual art cards, etc. Insider's delight. Closed Monday.

MUSEUM OF SCIENCE
Museum Park, Boston

One of the best places to be in Boston, a must for those with children. The museum is fabulous, and so is the store. Parents will appreciate the educational souvenirs.

NEW ENGLAND AQUARIUM
Central Wharf, Boston

Well, the aquarium is one of the best in the world, and surely one of Boston's most popular sights, but the gift shop is nothing to write home about.

Resale

THE CLOSET
175 Newbury St., Boston

There are several resale shops on Newbury but this is my favorite because this is the one where I scored. I found the most incredible Helmut Lang suit—perfect condition and in the latest style—for $139. It was even in my size! The store has Donna Karan cashmere, lots of designer names, and even a little bit of Chanel. Say your prayers, cross your fingers, and maybe today will be your lucky day.

THE BOSTON 'BURBS

Lexington

Although the names Lexington and Concord roll off the tongue in automatic twinship, the two cities are very, very different, especially to a shopper. Lexington looks, at first glance, like a great tourist city—with the green at the far end, a handful of picturesque colonial buildings, and a main street that offers row after row of stores.

It's only after you've walked that main street and been in each of those stores that you will find this is really a boring little town where no one seems to understand the needs of the visiting shopper. Basic tourist needs are met: You can buy postcards or an ice-cream cone. But satisfying? Exciting? Thrilling? You'll have to wait for Concord.

Concord

Concord is only 7 miles from Lexington, but when it comes to retail, the town is a million miles away and light years ahead. In contrast to Lexington, just about everything in Concord makes you itch to shop. This is just the kind of city where you want to wander in and out of the shops and enjoy a New England day. If you are combining Lexington and Concord into a one-day trip, as most people do, plan your time so that you prowl the stores of Concord and forget about Lexington shopping completely.

Concord shopping is not just devoted to a main-street strip, although you can pretty much walk to everything you want to see and shop. There are some freestanding stores around the rotary, away from the heaviest concentration of stores—so don't leave town too fast. You may come into town on Walden Street, shop Main Street, and then walk past the Colonial Tavern House to Monument Street for more shopping. Lexington Road, one of the spokes from the rotary, has more businesses on it and a tiny information booth.

Note that in the drive from Lexington to Concord you crossed the invisible area-code divide and are now in the 508 area code. You will have to dial 617 to reach Boston and the other 'burbs.

FINDS

APPLESEED'S
Monument St., Concord

Their stock-in-trade is the New England prep look, not so different from Talbot's. Their best items are sweaters with intricate Americana designs counted in: Some look like cross-stitch samplers. Prices are low to moderate. Call 800/767-6666 for a catalog or more information.

CONCORD ANTIQUES
Main St., Concord

Go down the stairs to a pleasant shop with country-style antiques and some linens and quilts. The feeling is nice, not haughty, though we found the prices a tad high.

CONCORD ANTIQUES COOP
23 Walden St., Concord

Upstairs, open 7 days a week from 10am to 7pm, Sunday noon to 5pm.

CONCORD MUSEUM SHOP
200 Lexington Rd., Concord

Specializing in New England crafts and decorative arts spread out over 15 restored rooms. They also have a lecture series and crafts lessons as well as— you guessed it—a gift shop.

THE FAMOUS CONCORD SHOP
23 Walden St., Concord

This little hodgepodge shop is an inviting brew of bottles, antiques, kitchen equipment, and the adjacent cheese shop.

THE NATURE COMPANY
15 Monument St., Concord

In a freestanding little house, this Nature Company has a very natural feel to it—the house adds a dimension of warmth that a mall just can't offer. The merchandise is the same Nature Company items we love from all their stores; there's plenty for children.

OPEN MARKET
28 Walden St., Concord

A melange of folk art, crafts, gifts, stuff, and imports that just has the wonderful look of great jumble and fun stuff. Touch it all.

Salem

If you think Salem is a sleepy little colonial village with a few witches hanging around, you are about 300 years behind the times. Salem is a good-sized city with a large downtown/tourist area and several trade neighborhoods for shoppers. While we're all quite quick to jump on the witch bandwagon, most of us have little idea of Salem's importance as a colonial port city. The books available are fascinating; the museums help you appreciate deep-water treasure.

Salem has been a shopping crossroads for centuries; its importance in shipping, government, and retail cannot be ignored by students of the trade arts. There are things of interest for the whole family. Salem is a city not to be ignored.

Oh, and did we mention? There's an antiques center right in town. So plan to spend a full day in Salem, if not more. There's so much to see and do and buy; you'll be sorry if you piggyback this stop with another.

THE LAY OF THE LAND

Because Salem is larger than you might anticipate, you may need some help getting oriented. Park centrally and find the visitor center, which is well stocked with books and materials. It is located on a red-line walking tour, much like Boston's Freedom Trail. The Witch Museums and related displays are at the edge of downtown and not in the main stream of things. The Peabody Museum makes a good central point; start your exploration of the town from there.

The Essex Street Mall is a pedestrian walkway that borders the Peabody on one side and hosts the National Park Service Visitor Information Center (open daily, 9am to 5pm, except January 1, Thanksgiving Day, and Christmas Day). From here you are only one block from the Essex Institute and can still walk to Pickering Wharf, a shopping development.

FINDS

PEABODY MUSEUM OF SALEM
East India Sq., Salem

The Peabody is a museum that celebrates deep-water treasure—all those items brought back on all those sailing ships that traversed the seas. There is a gift shop, although it's small and not terrific. The emphasis is on imported gifts that replicate treasures of the Orient, although we saw mostly cheap imports and a lot of good books about the Orient. The books are better than the gifts, but the museum as a whole is so wonderful you won't mind that the gift shop is not as good as the one at Mystic Seaport.

THE ESSEX INSTITUTE
132 Essex St., Salem

Another world-class museum, this one includes a series of houses and a lifestyle museum devoted to the decorative arts. The gift shop is tiny but crammed with the kinds of souvenirs and reproductions you associate with rich colonial times. There are a number of arts and crafts projects and some things for children. Admission to the museum shop is free. It's to your left as you enter the main door.

SALEM WITCH MUSEUM
Washington Sq., Salem

We don't want to be tacky, but we are really fired up for this place. Not only do they have a formal presentation, but they also have a large gift shop. The gifts celebrate the tercentenary (300-year anniversary) of the witch trials. There's also the usual in witch souvenirs, plus New England–oriented gifts and the usual lobster souvenirs. Good selection of books.

ANTIQUES GALLERY
Pickering Wharf, Salem

This is our kind of antiques place—lots of stands from lots of dealers, low to modest prices and some of them flexible. There's a wide range of goods here. Expect to stay for at least an hour and have a ball.

Rockport

Rockport is about an hour north of Boston on the North Shore. It is famous as an artists' community and has a number of touristy and crafty stores, offering a very nice day's or half-day's amusement. Rockport feels like a Norman Rockwell painting. There's the sea pounding at one corner and the little shops lined up on two shopping streets.

Rockport takes up the corner portion of what's really a little island between Ipswich Bay and Gloucester Harbor. The main shopping area is L-shaped, so that the center shopping street through town is Main Street, but you can then turn right onto Mount Pleasant Street for more shopping. Where the two meet there's a shopping strip called **Dockside Square.** Slightly further down, there's an adorable cluster of retail shops called **Bear Skin Neck.**

The most touristy shops are on Bear Skin Neck, but there are also some cute shops in converted houses, and some flower carts and seafood places that add to the wonderful seaside atmosphere. This is where you can stock up on T-shirts, crafts, tote bags, and resort wear.

FINDS

NEW ENGLAND GOODS
23 Main St., Rockport

With a name like this you are probably expecting a General Store, or some sort of TT. Actually, this is a very good crafts shop. Most of the work is done in wood; there are also some ceramics. Off to one side, an entire window is filled with colored-glass disks, imprinted with colonial designs, which reflect the light in a lovely rainbow. We think these are the perfect New England souvenirs and Christmas gifts. At $6 each we stocked up. We did see them later at crafts shops around New England and the Cape, but they were always more expensive.

SEA BOSTON AT ROCKPORT
Bear Skin Neck, Rockport

This is a T-shirt shop, but it has good graphics as well as some resort ready-to-wear, sunglasses, and totes.

TOAD HALL BOOKSTORE
51 Main St., Rockport

Excellent bookstore—the kind that makes you dream of retiring to a village like Rockport to read all day and stroll along the seawall.

Plymouth

Plymouth has far more shopping than the Pilgrims might ever have imagined, but is nonetheless rather grim—from a shopping standpoint, that is. For tourists, this place is fabulous. And your kids will love it. The scene here includes Plymouth, Plimoth, and Pilgrim, with the shopping emphasis on Tourist Trap. There is a big mall outside of town (shuttle available) and an outlet mall (boring) at the edge of town.

There are three main venues to Plymouth: the waterfront tourist area where you have the Rock, the central business district, and Plimoth Plantation, a historical re-creation, which is 2 miles away. If you are interested in the outlets, that's yet a fourth destination. You probably won't care about main-street shopping, and you're going to need a car to get around to the rest.

FINDS

PLIMOTH PLANTATION
Plymouth

We've been to a lot of lifestyle museums in our time—especially in the course of this book—but this is one of the best. The retail thrust is in the big house where you pay admission and can get a bite to eat (rest rooms too). This museum store still can't match Mystic, but it's pretty good.

PLIMOTH PLANTATION WATERFRONT SITE

Two of the best stores in all of Plymouth are in town, in the park near the Rock. They are run by the Plimoth Plantation people and they are wonderful. Both stores are in Pilgrim-style and offer a good selection of merchandise (although not as wide a selection as the museum shop).

CORDAGE PARK
Route 3A, Court St., Plymouth

This is a two-part marketplace of specialty stores and factory-outlet stores and they probably mean well, but after you have seen some of the other outlet stores, you realize this just isn't a very up-scale mall.

New Bedford

New Bedford has one of the fanciest factory-outlet malls in America, but this city has been a historical landmark for well over a hundred years because of the whaling business. Aside from a few blocks of delicious downtown—where a historic district offers limited retail, but much charm—New Bedford is large, sprawling, rather unattractive, and not too cheery. However, it has a great whaling museum, several scattered factory outlets, and a really fun antiques center. A day or two here will offer plenty of shopping opportunities.

New Bedford is about an hour from Newport, an hour from Boston, an hour from the Cape, and only a half hour from Providence. The city itself is quite large. Follow signs for "Historic District" (Exit 15 off I-95 East) to get to the whaling museum, the restored historic district, and the adjacent downtown where you will find the visitors' bureau for brochures and directions to the outlets. In some cases there are preprinted maps.

Expect to get lost; expect to feel like you are in the middle of nowhere as you drive off to Howland Place. Howland Place is in the middle of nowhere.

Note that if you really plan to dent all the outlets and get around town and see the Whaling Museum and see it all before you go broke, there is a tremendous amount of territory to cover from Fall River to New Bedford. If you only have one day, you'd better make choices before you even hit Fall River. (See page 58.)

FINDS

🛍 HOWLAND PLACE
651 Orchard St., New Bedford

You have a big psychological decision to make here: historic sites or bargains. Howland Place is the farthest tourist point out of town, so you might want to save it for the end of the day. But you want to have plenty of money on hand, so maybe you should go first thing. This is an outlet mall that has been changing because even in recession years it has already absorbed other nearby outlets; it is architecturally one of the fanciest malls in America and tends to have more high-end merchandise under one roof than any other mall.

New Bedford Antiques Company
85 Coggeshall St., New Bedford

Next door to an open-air flea market and farmer's market, this indoor center lives in the ground floor of an abandoned warehouse. Since most of the retail in New Bedford is in a factory or warehouse, this will not strike you as strange. There are over 200 dealers in rows of stalls in this redbrick building offering a variety of things, most with a country theme. There's some 1950s stuff, but not a lot. At the door you can also get brochures about nearby fairs and events. Open Monday through Saturday, 10am to 5pm; Sunday, noon to 5pm. This is not far from the Calvin Klein outlet, if you are organizing your adventure in any particular order.

Chapter Nine

· · · · · · ·

CAPE COD, NANTUCKET & MARTHA'S VINEYARD

CAPE COD CONFESSIONS

· ·

I am about to blurt this out on the rare chance that it will happen to you and that no one else you know will make such a confession: Cape Cod is a mysterious place.

It's a mystery to me how the words "Cape Cod" can evoke so much energy and enthusiasm from so many people who react as if all parts of the Cape are created equal and will be equally divine. Phew! I've said it; I feel years younger.

Cape Cod can be wonderful or awful; be suspicious of anyone who loves *all* of it.

To me, Cape Cod is a hard nut to crack. It took us many, many trips to find the good places—which are really hidden—to get a sense of privacy and peace. Sure, if you know the drill, have some money, know how to find the privacy and the perfection, there's a spiritual thing that might carry over into the rest of your life. If you come as a first-timer or a tourist, golly gee, look out: A lot of the Cape is crass, commercial, overpopulated in summer, and not unlike parts of the Caribbean.

My original Cape Cod fantasy was to drive around, see some gorgeous houses and scenery and flowers, and stop at antiques shops and fairs and auctions and cute little villages. With no small amount of effort we were able to live that fantasy—in some towns. We hope to steer you to those charming hamlets, and away from the crass commercialism that is threatening to take over Massachusetts's lovely seashore. I simply hated a lot of Cape Cod.

THE LAY OF THE LAND

Cape Cod is the name of the J-shaped peninsula of land that juts off the side of Massachusetts creating one of the most noticeable landmarks on the map of the U.S. Technically, it is separated from the mainland by the Cape Cod Canal and is in fact a freestanding island. You gain access by crossing one of the two almost identical bridges over the canal.

The Cape is divided into three regions, each made up of towns and villages and beaches and shopping opportunities of various sizes and shapes. There is the Upper Cape, Mid-Cape, and Lower Cape. The uppermost portion of the Cape on the map, the one furthest away from the canal, is the Lower Cape. The one closest to the canal is the Upper Cape. Go figure.

Your goal on your first visit to Cape Cod should be to use it as a learning experience to find the right place for future family trips. Explore the back routes and individual villages to get an understanding of their personalities. Eventually, we promise, the jumble of villages that comprise Cape Cod will begin to make sense to you.

GETTING THERE

By Plane

There is an airport in Hyannis (Barnstable Municipal Airport to be exact. Note the lack of the word international in the name; this should be a clue as to the size of this airport). If you want to fly to the Cape and land on a bigger piece of runway, you can fly right into the Providence airport, now being serviced by several big-name but low-priced airlines, such as Delta Express and Southwest. The Providence airport is the largest "real" airport in the area, shy of Boston.

By Ferry

You can take a ferry from Plymouth or Boston to Provincetown, the farthest town on the Lower Cape. You can also ferry to the Islands (Nantucket and Martha's Vineyard) from the mainland. If you are going to the Cape and then on to Nantucket or Martha's Vineyard, make reservations for your car on the ferry as far in advance as possible. (**Steamship Authority** is the line that accommodates cars; ☎ 508/477-8600). Or plan to leave your car in one of the many lots encircling the two different ferry terminals.

There are a number of ferry lines and various ports of departure, so it can be confusing. Only Steamship Authority carries cars from Hyannis. Make sure you arrive and depart on the same line and get back to the right town. You will not be pleased if you leave your car in Hyannis but take a ferry back to New Bedford.

By Bus

There is frequent bus service from Boston and Logan International Airport in Boston. Buses head for Bourne, Falmouth, and Woods Hole. Call Bonanza (800/556-3815) for bus info.

By Train

Amtrak offers summer service on what they call the Cape Codder, a train from New York, Philadelphia, and Washington, (and points en route) that

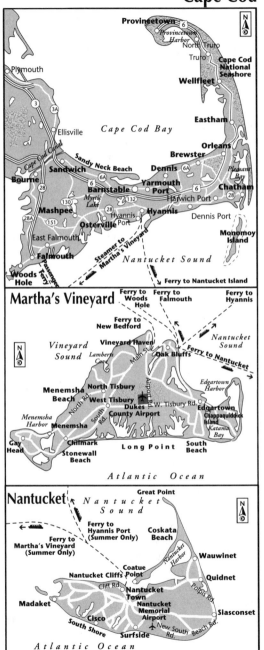

Cape Cod

N

Provincetown
Provincetown Harbor
North Truro
Truro
Cape Cod National Seashore
Plymouth
Wellfleet
3
3A
Eastham
Cape Cod Bay
Ellisville
Orleans
Brewster
Sandy Neck Beach
Pleasant Bay
6A
Dennis
Bourne
Sandwich
6A
Yarmouth Port
Chatham
28
Barnstable
6
Myrtic Lake
132
Harwich Port
28
130
Mashpee
28
Hyannis Port
Hyannis
Dennis Port
151
Osterville
Monomoy Island
East Falmouth
Steamer to Martha's Vineyard
Nantucket Sound
Falmouth
Woods Hole
passenger
↘ **Ferry to Nantucket Island**

Martha's Vineyard

N

Ferry to Woods Hole
Ferry to Falmouth
Ferry to Hyannis
Ferry to New Bedford
Vineyard Sound
Nantucket Sound
Vineyard Haven
Lamberts Cove
Main St.
Oak Bluffs
Ferry to Nantucket
Menemsha Beach
North Tisbury
North Rd.
Airport Rd.
Edgartown Harbor
West Tisbury
South Rd.
Dukes County Airport
S. W. Tisbury Rd.
Edgartown
Menemsha Harbor
Menemsha
Chilmark
Chappaquiddick Island
Katama Bay
Gay Head
Stonewall Beach
Long Point
South Beach
Atlantic Ocean

Nantucket

Great Point
Nantucket Sound
N
Ferry to Hyannis Port (Summer Only)
Coskata Beach
Ferry to Martha's Vineyard (Summer Only)
Nantucket Harbor
Wauwinet
Coatue Point
Nantucket Cliffs
Cliff Rd.
Quidnet
Polpis Rd.
Nantucket Town
Madaket
Nantucket Memorial Airport
Siasconset
Cisco
New South Rd.
Beach Rd.
South Shore
Surfside
Atlantic Ocean

branches off after Providence to service Sandwich, West Barnstable, and Hyannis, all points on the Cape. Sometimes you must transfer to bus service. Call 800/USA-RAIL for details.

By Car

Because the area is such an enormous tourist destination, try to avoid driving across either of the bridges during peak travel times, especially in summer. Also try to avoid the Friday afternoon/early evening migration to the Cape and the Sunday evening exodus. The Cape has a main highway (Route 6) that runs right up the center of the peninsula, making it a very easy and relatively quick way to get around. We prefer driving the back roads: Route 28 for the southern part of the Cape and Route 6A for the northern part. Both offer all the charm you want and expect. Free maps are abundant and will show you how to get across sections of the peninsula. Traffic can be bumper to bumper, even on Route 6.

SLEEPING THE CAPE
. . . .

Finding the right hotel, motel, cabin, or B&B for your personal tastes is not easy in Cape Cod. This is one of the reasons we suggest you consider your first trip here an exploratory one. You'll probably want to inspect a lot of different properties and take notes for your next visit. Hyannis is the commercial heart of Cape Cod; just about every big hotel chain is represented. These places are convenient, well priced, and clean, but they aren't charming and are located on a busy highway.

B&B's or inns are a much more personal matter. We recommend you solicit the advice of friends or relatives with similar tastes who have visited the Cape and found places they've enjoyed.

BEST BUYS OF THE CAPE

· ·

Antiques: I can't say that the antiques are a steal, that you must rush to this area for a bargain, that no one else is on to the scene. The truth is the dealers are here in droves and every fair is well attended. The shops vary from poor to very, very good. There are also tag sales, flea markets, yard sales, and auctions. The two biggest flea markets are in Wellfleet, in the parking lot of a drive-in movie theater (300 dealers) and another market known as Dick & Ellie's, on Route 28 in Mashpee, which gets about 100 dealers.

Beach Needs: There are plenty of discounters and off-pricers to sell you any beach needs you may have, from clothing to towels to boogie boards and more.

Art: I'm not a very good judge of this because I rarely go into galleries and I'm not the kind of person who puts money into things that go on the wall. I invest in shoes. But enough about me. There are scads of art galleries in Cape Cod; obviously all schools of art abound. There's a specialty in lighthouses and seascapes and Victorian scenics and etchings. Must be something in the water.

Factory Outlets: There are a rather large number of outlets sprinkled around the Cape. Some are free-standing, such as the Dansk outlet in Hyannis (see page 43); some are fake—most easily categorized by the dozens of so-called "T-shirt factory outlets" that pop up everywhere. There's a fair-sized outlet mall in Sagamore and a tiny strip at the Bourne Rotary. Both of these are excellent. The **Cape Cod Factory Outlet Mall** and **Tanger Factory Outlet Center** are also worth checking out.

Souvenirs: If you're looking for silly gifts to take back to your friends, those coffee mugs with the lobster-shaped handle can be found in any of the millions of tourist-trap shops scattered all over the Cape. Prices for souvenirs on the Cape are far better than on Nantucket or Martha's Vineyard. There are T-shirt "factories" where shirts are sold from bins and cost $2 to $5. Shirts range from the worst quality and design (least expensive) to the best (about $15); if you are traveling with children who can read, you might want to steer clear of some of the T-shirt shops in Provincetown. Or be prepared to answer some sexually explicit questions.

Christmas: It must be Christmas all year round, or certainly during the "season" in Cape Cod, since Christmas-decoration stores are the rage. There are zillions of them.

HOURS

Hours vary a little bit from town to town and according to the local interest in retail. Most cities have some Sunday shopping, but it can be spotty or limited to the bigger tourist cities and the malls. Stores may move to reduced hours out of season or may completely close shop. Several of the antiques dealers have stores in Florida and spend winters there. You'll find many in Dania, near Fort Lauderdale!

MONEY MATTERS

I found very few retailers willing to take the American Express card. This was not true in Nantucket and Martha's Vineyard, but was generally the rule in every town on Cape Cod. ATM machines are found everywhere, so you can get cash as needed. Call **Cape Cod Bank & Trust** at 800/458-5100 for the addresses of their 28 Cape Cod branches.

THE UPPER CAPE

The Upper Cape is the part you come to as soon as you cross the canal. The main cities are Bourne,

Falmouth, Mashpee, and Sandwich. The spirit of the Cape actually begins before you cross over the bridge and into Bourne. By the time you get to Buzzards Bay, with its miniature golf, batting cages, lobster joints, inflatable water-toy emporiums, and nurseries selling lobster buoys, you'll know you have arrived. By the time you get to Bourne and its London Bridge tower, you'll have had enough of the commercial Cape and be ready to get on Route 28 and head south, toward the good stuff . . . or north, and onto Route 6A and more good stuff. Since the Upper Cape is closest to Boston and civilization, it is also the most developed. You're going to have to hit the back roads to find country charm. Sandwich is a pretty colonial town, but not a great shopping city. Falmouth and Mashpee have everything you might want to shop for.

Sandwich

You might think of it as something to eat; I think of it as the home of American glass. This is a cutie-pie town with some good galleries and shops . . . and the famous glass museum. The Sandwich Auction House is a local favorite, even among residents. The Sandwich Antiques Center, 131 Rte. 6A, has 150 dealers and is open daily, from 10am to 6pm.

FINDS

SANDWICH LANTERN
17 Jan Sebastian Way, #16, Sandwich

Fabulously creative lanterns with handblown local glass, natch. Call 800/966-9443 for more info.

SNOW GOOSE SHOP
Merchants Sq., Rte. 6A, Sandwich

Store filled with local cutie-pie and country looks, including more of the local lanterns and pieces of glass. Open daily, 9am to 5pm.

GLASS STUDIO/MICHAEL MAGYAR
470 Rte. 6A, Sandwich

Private studio of local glassblower; open daily,
10am to 5pm.

BROWN JUG
Main St., Sandwich

Did someone say cranberry glass?

COLLECTIONS UNLIMITED
Rte. 6A, East Sandwich

Cooperative of 25 local artists. Closed in January.

Mashpee

Those who are interested in retail history will high-
tail it over to Mashpee, where shopping historians
are busy taking notes. There was a mall in Mashpee
called the New Seabury Shopping Center. It was
bought, torn down, and in its place a small shopping village called **Mashpee Commons** was built—
and it is magical. The village is a bit like a Disney
town, all adorable architecture and manufactured
charm. There are places to eat, and a bank and a
hardware store and a few other basic shops for locals. Then there are a few big-name branch stores
like The Gap and local retailers like **Irresistibles.** I'm
big on hand-painted furniture, so I adore **Painted
Treasures.** Open Monday through Friday, 10am
to 8pm; Saturday, 10am to 9pm; Sunday, noon
to 5pm. Located at the Mashpee Rotary, intersec-
tion of Routes 28 and 151.

Falmouth

Falmouth is one of those storybook New England
villages, one of the places you have dreamed about
visiting. It has a traditional town green, a few
historic houses, and a main street for strolling and
shopping. Many of the stores are TTs, but if this is

your first introduction to shopping in Cape Cod, even the TTs are fresh and fun.

FINDS

CALINE FOR KIDS
149 Main St., Falmouth

Adorable shop with an excellent blend of the clothes grandmothers can't stop buying and fun beach gear for the kiddies.

FENCE RAIL
233 Main St., Falmouth

A ready-to-wear shop for women that sells mostly resort clothes and some preppy looks, but also has gifts and Salt Marsh Pottery, an earthenware with dried flowers pressed into it.

MARSHMALLOW
193 Main St., Falmouth

New quilts, canvas chairs, kitchen and entertaining needs sold in an environment of style and class. It looks like something out of the pages of a magazine, but locals consider it the neighborhood equivalent of Pottery Barn.

Woods Hole

So you're taking the ferry from Woods Hole and figured you'd browse around and do a little shopping before getting on board. Wrong. Downtown Woods Hole is very quaint and unspoiled by tourism, but there's not much to buy here. Stop by **Under the Sun,** 22 Water St., just to poke around and look at crafts.

Osterville

You're approaching Mid-Cape as you head through this fairy-tale hamlet that's slightly off the beaten track, where we promise you'll have a great time moseying around and browsing. This is the village we hope to retire to—it's upscale and jazzy without being one bit touristy. Don't miss **Claire Murray,** my queen of hooked carpets, 867 Main St., or catch her in Nantucket (see page 212).

THE MID-CAPE

This is the narrower part of the hood of land, before it turns up in the backwards J–shape; it is the longest of the three segments and the one offering the most contrast, from bustling Hyannis to serene Yarmouth Port. The main towns in this area are Barnstable, Yarmouth, Dennis, Brewster, Harwich, Chatham, and Hyannis. The only way to enjoy the Mid-Cape is by car and without a schedule. Take those country roads and just drive. Stop to shop, to poke into antiques markets, to browse local fairs and flea markets. It's an idyllic adventure.

Route 6A

Heaven. We feel like we have died and gone to heaven when we find ourselves driving from Orleans toward Sandwich on Route 6A. We ignore those local drivers riding our bumper behind us who take it all for granted. We just want to drive slowly, stare at the beautiful houses, memorize the colors of the wildflower gardens, and pull over every now and then for any special shops that catch our eye.

Chatham

Located in the far corner of the Mid-Cape, Chatham is a very independent village with a lot of charm to it—and a lot of shopping. It's a pretty big town with a number of places you might want to stop to shop, although its downtown 1-mile shopping stretch on Main Street is its claim to fame.

FINDS

CHATHAM HARDWARE
624 Main St., Chatham

A good resource for Cape Cod–style gifts: sailing and marine-oriented items, birdbaths, weathervanes, tide clocks, etc.

THE LION'S PAW
436 Main St., Chatham

Good taste in housewares and gifts and table arts. Not as extravagant as the one in Nantucket, but an excellent store nonetheless.

UNIQUES, LTD.
Main St., Chatham

I can't tell you this is the best shop in town, but we went nuts for their weathervanes. The country gifts are OK, but the weathervanes are terrific and well-priced, too. These are new (made in the Orient), but are well-crafted and heavy. Prices range from $85 to $105, which is very fair.

Hyannis

If you grew up in the age of Camelot, you probably associate Hyannis with the Kennedy family. Actually, their famous compound is in Hyannisport. Hyannis is another story—it's the big commercial city in Cape Cod: home of the airport; home of a commercial drag filled with motels, fast-food eateries, and shopping centers; home to the main ferry terminals; and gateway to the Islands. If you need something, this is where you go. If you are looking for charm, it is not.

There are three areas to Hyannis where you can find three different types of shopping.

Main Street has an old-fashioned retail area that's really pretty ordinary (sometimes the church has a crafts sale), and a touristy section where every store on both sides of the street sells local souvenirs. This two-block stretch ends at the **Antique Co-Op,** which is in a former grocery store. Next door to this is the **Hyannis Indoor Flea Market,** which is exceptionally junky and may spill over into the parking lot. You can buy T-shirts and souvenirs as well as beach needs for cheap. Next door are the **Hyannis Factory Outlets,** a small strip that does not have anything you should drive out of your way to see.

Route 132 is the lifeblood of the retail business. This is where the fast-food chains, the hotel chains, and big stores are located. The stores are in strip centers or malls, all in a row beginning at the rotary right in front of the entrance to the airport and leading away from Hyannis toward Route 6. The densest part of the shopping is between the rotary and the Cape Cod Mall, less than a mile in distance.

The Steamship Authority is located on **South Street;** Hy-Line is around the corner on **Ocean Street.** There are tourist kiosks selling film, books, and souvenirs, but otherwise you'll have to drive for retail. There are places to eat within walking distance of each terminal.

FINDS

CHRISTMAS TREE PROMENADE
Rte. 132, Hyannis

There are a lot of Christmas shops in Hyannis, and you will quickly forget which ones you've been to. No matter; this one is still a must.

COLONIAL CANDLE
232 Main St., Hyannis

Although candle places are a dime a dozen in New England, this is the best one in Cape Cod (there are other branch locations). The flagship shop is in Hyannis in a compound made up of several white colonial-style buildings. One is an outlet store where

Local Potters

Salt Marsh Pottery
115 Main St., Wellfleet

Earthenware with flowers pressed into it.

Wellfleet Pottery
165 Commercial St., Wellfleet

Two different styles here, both done in almost country-French hues like soft-green or ochre. There are solids with color inside and earthenware (unglazed) on the outside and then there's simple little florals painted across a piece.

Kemp Pottery
Rte. 6A, Orleans

Decorative stonewares and household items.

Chilmark Pottery
145 Field View Lane, West Tisbury

Mostly inspired by Japanese techniques, including but not limited to raku, this potter has his studio on Martha's Vineyard where you can stop by and visit and shop his barnyard studio. He's open daily, 9:30am to 6pm.

Chatham Pottery
2058 Main St. (Rte. 28), South Chatham

House specialty is a blue-and-white that's very mother-earthy; fish motifs are common, but not the cutie-pie kiddie fish—these are almost Japanese in a koi manner and are very sophisticated.

Scargo Pottery
Rte. 6A, Dennis

Actually this is right off the road at Dr. Lord's Road South; an entire pottery family doing very whimsical things, including elaborate birdhouses. Open daily, 10am to 5pm.

Heart Pottery
1145 Rte. 6A, Brewster

Local potter makes good; all at home on the wheel with unusual floral designs.

they sell toys and silly, small gifts as well as candles. In the main store, there are candles of every flavor and scent imaginable. This is where Aaron once spotted an Oreo-shaped candle ($10) he hasn't stopped talking about. Open daily.

THE LOWER CAPE

· ·

When the land mass turns up into the Bay and the side roads cease to exist, you're headed into the Lower Cape, which dead-ends in Provincetown, known as P-town. The most commercial points of the area are Orleans and P-town, but between them you'll find Eastham, Wellfleet, and Truro. This is the most unspoiled part of the Cape, the least commercial in terms of big shopping opportunities (although P-town has more than its share of shopping choices).

Orleans is only about 10 miles south of Chatham, so again the border between points becomes a blur. Orleans has mostly "real-people" shopping with stores like **Bradlees** and several supermarkets.

Wellfleet

Wellfleet is known as the artsy, antiquey center of the Lower Cape. Just outside Eastham, at the Wellfleet Drive-In, you can start your shopping on Saturday and Sunday at a flea market that sprawls across half the parking lot. Although admission is $1 per car, there are free-admission coupons in all of the tourist literature. The flea market features mostly new merchandise; in the back, to the right, some people have taken space for a tag-sale type of event. Only a few of the 300 vendors are serious dealers; prices should be carefully negotiated.

Once you are in downtown Wellfleet, there are several galleries for crafts and antiques. It's a nice browse, but this is not one of those villages that will knock you over with selection. There's a handful of shops. Some we like are **The Wellfleet Collection**

(Baker Avenue), **The Secret Garden** (Main Street), and **Finders Keepers** (Main Street and Briar Lane, enter on the side of the barn). **Salt Marsh Pottery** is at 115 Main St. (see page 197).

Provincetown

Provincetown is the scenic part of the Lower Cape, with the kind of tourist scene you don't mind because it's just so perfect. It has a circus atmosphere of fun that no other village on the Cape has, which is a part of the local charm. P-town is the big show.

Parking can be hard to come by; the main lots are filled by 11am in the summer. Get to town early. **MacMillan Wharf** is the center of the action—you get on the boat for the whale-watching cruise here—and the shopping is off to each side on the main street, called, aptly enough, Commercial Street.

The main shopping area is abuzz with T-shirt shops, taffy shops, artists who draw caricatures and portraits, little malls, flower carts, and Oriental imports. There are kites and color and whales and celebrations everywhere you look.

P-town is a year-round community; it is delightful off-season. Enough stores are open year-round to make this a fun town to shop any season of the year.

Provincetown has a large gay population and is visited by a lot of gay tourists. We mention this only because there are some very explicit T-shirts for sale; we got a lot of questions from Aaron that we were unprepared for. "I'm not gay, but my boyfriend is" T-shirts are the least of it.

FINDS

CROSSYAFINGAS
191 Commercial St., Provincetown

Say it out loud and laugh and enjoy this tiny, but very hip, ready-to-wear shop. Despite some Indian imports, this store has tremendous flair and high style.

IMPULSE
188 Commercial St., Provincetown

Excellent crafts shop. Photography featured in the rear.

MARINE SPECIALTIES
235 Commercial St., Provincetown

This is the kind of store the kids will love. Most of the merchandise is marine surplus and not that exciting, but the setting is so much fun that you—and everyone in the family—will have a ball exploring this shop.

PORT OF CALL
MacMillan Wharf, Provincetown

One of the leading wharf shops for beach and surfer fashions, boogie boards, neon hats and baggies, camera cases, sweats, and flip-flops.

THE WILDLIFE WORKSHOP
350 Commercial St., Provincetown

Environmental gifts. Couldn't get greener. Come here after your whale watch to feel completely ecologically correct.

WELCOME TO THE ISLANDS

I admit to being confused the first time we saw the road sign indicating THE ISLANDS. We didn't think we were that close to the Caribbean. We've certainly never heard anyone say, "I'm going to the Islands," and actually mean they were going to Martha's Vineyard or Nantucket, but maybe we don't know the right people.

The two islands are so dramatically different that those visiting one specific island for more than a weekend should find a way to manage to ferry across and spend a day poking (and shopping) around on the other.

NANTUCKET

. . . .

Hmmmm, I wish I could find it in my heart to give you a warm, enthusiastic welcome to Nantucket, but I really don't want you to come . . . because then you, too, will realize the secret locals are so jealously guarding: Nantucket is a very special place.

Come if you must to dress up, shop up, and eat up. But when you return home, don't let anyone know that there really is no reason to go to Europe, to seek the hot spots of the world, to look beyond the next yacht—because it's all right here.

Nantucket is a rather small island some 2 hours by ferry from Hyannis. The main town, called "town" by locals, is named Nantucket, the same as the island. This is not as confusing as it may seem, since the other towns are known by their names, and streets can only be so long on the island. There is no shopping to speak of outside of town; see the neighborhoods section on page 205.

Getting There/Getting Around

Since Nantucket is an island, you have limited options here. You can fly in; you can ferry in. (Of course, you can always yacht in.) There are two piers serving the ferry companies (**Hy-Line** and the **Steamship Authority**) that come to Nantucket from the mainland and from Martha's Vineyard. Service to and from Martha's Vineyard is seasonal; service to the mainland is regular, weather permitting.

If you're bringing a car to Nantucket, you will need a reservation. Only one of the ferry lines (Steamship Authority) accepts cars. Space goes quickly, especially for Saturdays. Local residents get first dibs, then the public. By April (prior to the season), ferry openings can be hard to come by.

When you make your reservation to get on the island, make sure to make one to get off. When departing the island, you can sometimes send your car ahead of you the night before your own departure—it will be waiting for you at the ferry terminal in Hyannis.

Both ferry terminals are convenient to downtown; if you have a lot of luggage and no car, you will want to get a cab to your hotel.

Getting around Nantucket is simple. See those two feet attached to your body? They will propel your body, or your bike, every place you need to go. Unless you are staying at the Wauwinet. Then you need a car.

If you need a cab, call Atlantic Cabs (☎ 508/228-1122). From Boston, call 800/444-1511 to arrange connecting service.

If you park your car on the mainland, note that lots are less expensive as you move away from the terminal, few lots have guards, and rates are for the calendar day, not a 24-hour period.

Hours, Addresses & Attire

Stores open between 9am and 10am; some even open that early on Sunday. Sunday is a big day for retail during the season, but Sunday shopping dries up at 5pm sharp. Every other evening, the stores are open until at least 9pm. Some are open later.

While most stores are in houses that have been converted to retail but retain their street numbers, it is common for stores to list their addresses in ads, phone books, and on business cards as just the street name—no number given. Don't panic. This is a test. You're just supposed to know. If you can't find what you are looking for, simply ask.

One other note: You can go shopping any which way you please—even in a bathing suit with a pair of shorts pulled over your bottom. But do not go to dinner in a state of disarray. In Nantucket, one dresses for dinner and the window shopping stroll that follows. Casual, upscale dress will do.

Nantucket Style

Books have been written on Nantucket style. Most of them focus on the home and refer to either the formal brick Federal homes, the beach cottages overgrown with roses, or the neoclassical wooden houses located so close to the street you can sometimes sneak a peek through the drawing-room windows or see into the gardens and yards. Nantucket style extends from the houses onto the streets, into the store windows, and of course to the patrons. In fact, Nantucket is a real insider's kind of place, and understanding their unwritten rules of style will help you assimilate.

There is, in fact, a silent dress code—a method of communication that tells others you belong on the island. You'll find that the shops cater to this look, so if you suddenly feel uncomfortable with your wardrobe, fix yourself up in one of these looks:

- **The Rich Island Look:** For women, a very, very expensive hand-knit sweater will do; one-of-a-kind is preferred. Cashmere will do, especially in a fabulous, plush summer color and with matching outfit or shawl or in a twin set. Wear the extra sweater casually thrown over the shoulders with a plain white men's T-shirt, jeans, khakis, or white cotton slacks or shorts. Shoes can be ballet shoes, Chanel flats, Cole-Haan mocs, or leather sandals. Carry either a lightship basket or a Dooney & Bourke bag in a pinch. Men, see the Traditional Preppy look below.
- **The Traditional Preppy:** This look is alive and well all over New England and in the U.S. Those who don't have the look in their blood can always go to a Polo/Ralph Lauren shop. To garner the local version, be sure you wear your

Nantucket Reds, trousers made from stone-washed red fabric. Men: No socks with those mocs or Top-Siders, please.

- **Earthy Prep:** This is the 1990s version of preppy that no one over 40 wears but does tolerate in one's children—it's the traditional preppy look meets the 1960s flower child. Wear ethnic shirts from India with jeans (or Reds). Acceptable variation for hot weather: college-logo T-shirt teamed with printed or plaid boxer shorts. Baseball cap (worn backwards OK), mocs without socks, straw tote bag or L. L. Bean backpack.

- **Caribbean Chic:** It's totally acceptable to wear batik, seashell designs, and the kinds of clothes you would not wear on the Cape or in many other American resorts (except maybe Florida) because they are too, well, too much. Big loose sundresses, floppy straw hats in coordinated colors, plastic shell charm bracelets—all acceptable.

Only in Nantucket

Now that you know how chichi Nantucket can be, we know you'll want your own Nantucket Card—a Visa card with a picture of the island of Nantucket on it. Pacific National Bank issues them: Apply on Main Street or call 508/228-1917.

If you didn't go for the Nantucket Card, perhaps you'd like to invest instead in a meadow muffin. If you are uninformed, a meadow muffin is what we used to call a road apple in our part of the woods. You buy a piece of land for a $10 charitable donation; on Meadow Muffin Megabucks Day, any muffin on your "property" is worth a cash prize. The rest goes to charity. Ask at Island Pharmacy or Nantucket Pharmacy, both on Main Street.

Nantucket Seasons

There is summer season, from Memorial Day through Labor Day, and then there is The Season:

from Daffodil Days (in April) through Christmas Stroll (in December). Summer population on the island is about 40,000—five times the winter populace. The year is really divided between summer visitors, part-timers (April through December), and year-rounders. Those who live on-island on a part-time basis will leave before the Christmas rush (but after the cranberry harvest) or shortly after the new year begins, and return in April.

Another important season is Sale Season. Things begin to go on sale around the end of August and will be marked down to about half price.

Nantucket Neighborhoods

Wharves: If you take the Hy-Line ferry you will arrive at a wharf and immediately be tossed into Touristville. Stores, taverns, and shopping possibilities abound. You are at the Straight Wharf. Walk straight ahead to town and Straight Wharf becomes Main Street. If you come off Straight Wharf, turn left and then left again, you will be on Old South Wharf. You will be bounded by water and surrounded by shopping, crafts, eateries, yachts, and high style. Note that some of the retailers are regulars and some come and go each season.

Easy Street: Anyone who can vacation on Nantucket does live on Easy Street. Now you can shop Easy Street. If you want to see some shops slightly off the beaten path, if you want to check out the White Elephant, or Harbor House, then stroll toward Steamship Wharf—the other wharf for ferries—on Easy Street, and take in the stores as well.

Petticoat Lane: Although Main Street is the primary shopping drag of downtown, there is a grid of several shopping streets, mostly north of Main Street. The area surrounded by Centre, South Water, Main, and Broad streets will offer tons of cute shops to explore. Centre Street was once called Petticoat Row because of the number of stores run by women. I call the whole area Petticoat Lane.

Main Street: It's wide, it has cobblestones in one portion, and it's the heart of the city. Even at night, especially on warm summer nights, it buzzes with action. After Centre Street, Main Street becomes mostly residential. And what houses! Be sure to walk around even after the stores shut down. Main Street also plays host to area farmers who set up trucks and sell produce and flowers every morning except Sunday.

Best Buys of Nantucket

Hand-knit Sweaters: Because of the climate, sweaters are often worn in the evenings in Nantucket. The variety of ready-to-wear shops stock tons of sweaters in all categories, styles, prices, and fibers. When they go on sale, you can even get a bargain. The selection of unique sweaters is so great that even those who pride themselves on avoiding a cookie-cutter look may want to stock up while in town.

Hooked Rugs: Although Claire Murray is the local big name in hooked rugs, you can buy new versions of this colonial art in many shops in town—so many shops, that you will have a very good selection to choose from. New rugs are usually imported and cost between $100 and $400. You can also make your own, from scratch or a kit.

Lightship Baskets: Originally made by men who sat on lightships—floating lighthouses. Lightship baskets are an industry for craftspeople and a status symbol for fashionable ladies. Today you can buy an antique, buy one made by a craftsperson, or even make your own. The basket is most often round or oval, with a leather hinge to attach the top, and is fastened with a loop and peg. The peg is made of ivory. The top of the basket is a wooden disk on which a carved ivory decoration is placed. The basket should not be lined; it should be signed. It may also have a penny glued to the bottom with the date showing, indicating the year the basket was made. Such a basket should last for centuries. Expect to pay about $1,000 for a new basket; $2,000 for an old basket; $3,000 (and up) for an unusual basket. You can get a "fake" for about $150. At the Nantucket airport they have imitations for $60, the least expensive in town, but one look tells you they're frauds.

Nantucket Reds: One of the status symbols of Nantucket is clothing made from a rusty-red fabric called Nantucket Red. The true Nantucket Red is stonewashed and faded and comes from Murray's (see page 214), which has copyrighted the name. You can buy shorts, pants, wrap skirts, and baseball caps from this famous fabric, which indicates to observers that you are "in." The older and more faded your Reds, the better. While there are competing goods, true believers will only buy from Murray's.

Nantucket Resources

ANTIQUES

BON TON
Cambridge St., Nantucket

It's a shack! But it's crammed with fun stuff—some of it not worth the asking price. Who cares? It's a bargain if you luck out. Look for Cambridge Street in the web of little side streets near South Water Street.

FORAGER HOUSE
20 Centre St., Nantucket

Architectural artworks; folk art for the collector.

NINA HELLMAN
48 Centre St., Nantucket

Marine antiques is the house specialty, but there are other folk arts as well. Small selection in two parlor rooms of an old house.

KALEIDOSCOPE
42 Centre St., Nantucket

English and French-country furniture, decorative arts, fabrics, rugs and baskets, Marseilles weave, and some toys, but mostly a source for big pieces of pine furniture. Good luck getting it on the ferry with you.

WAYNE PRATT
6 Candle St., Nantucket

This fancy main-street store should not intimidate you; go in and enjoy. Take a free postcard—they're the best in Nantucket. The look is country colonial.

TONKIN OF NANTUCKET
33 Main St., Nantucket

Fabulous! Lightship baskets, tons of furniture, and small items; this crammed store is more fun than your last birthday.

AUCTIONS

Call Rafael Osuna (☎ 508/228-3942) for the dates of his summer auctions.

BASIC NEEDS

AUNT LEAH'S
The Courtyard, Straight Wharf, Nantucket

Sells fudge and candy, jams and condiments; the cranberry honey makes a great gift. In a mini-mall called the Courtyard. Major teen and kid hangout. Low-fat for grown-ups.

FOUR WINDS
Straight Wharf, Nantucket

This is the first stop on your stroll from Straight Wharf to Main Street; it's also the best, the most major, the most exciting, the most enticing tourist trap in town. This is the general store for all your needs. There are bins of inexpensive toys and souvenirs to keep kids happy; there are dishes and more serious souvenirs to please adults.

May win the prize for best "fake" lightship baskets in Nantucket because the color is good, and the baskets are unlined. A penny is even glued to the bottom with the date up so you always know the vintage.

HARDY'S
13 S. Water St., Nantucket

The local hardware store selling a little of everything including "fake" lightship baskets, postcards, beach needs, toys for the kids, and artist supplies. Closed Sunday.

SUNKEN SHIP
Broad St., Nantucket

This store, slightly off the beaten path, sells jeans, beach and sailing needs, and plenty of souvenirs. Come here for your fishing rods, your foul-weather gear, or your croquet set.

BASKETS (LIGHTSHIP)

THE LIGHTSHIP SHOP
20 Miacomet Ave., Nantucket

Husband-and-wife team; baskets are an affordable $200!

RICHARD & PATRICIA ANDERSON
9 Old South Wharf, Nantucket

Nantucket lightship baskets are made by this husband-and-wife team.

G. L. BROWN
1 Old South Wharf, Nantucket

Gerald Brown is a local craftsman known for his signed baskets.

FOUR WINDS CRAFT GUILD
6 Straight Wharf, Nantucket

Start your education into the art of lightship baskets right at the wharf in Nantucket in this long, narrow shop that seems to be a gallery. The patient staff will teach you all the ins and outs of weaving, will show you the difference between an apprentice and a master's basket, and will sell you the various parts to piece together your own finished basket. Expect to pay at least $1,000 (but closer to $1,350 for something special).

This is near but not quite next door to the TT of the same name and ownership. Don't get them confused; do enjoy both.

BOOKS

THE HUB
31 Main St., Nantucket

Good source for paperbacks, but best known as the place to buy newspapers and magazines. On Sunday mornings, stop in for your paper and check out the scene. Be prepared to be seen as well.

MITCHELL'S BOOK CORNER
54 Main St., Nantucket

A house of books that seems stiff and literary-minded when you first wander in, but which does stock plenty of good reading and a heavy-duty supply of "beach books." They go deep on best-selling paperbacks for the summer season. A lot of their material is related to local interests and history. Everyone comes by and hangs out.

Home Style

 ### April Cornell/Handblock
42 Main St., Nantucket

Most of the Handblock stores I shop in have changed their name to April Cornell, which is the name of the owner and designer. As far as I'm concerned, it's about time she got some credit and this is a name to remember. I buy tons from here; every year I get more tablecloths, place mats, pillowcases, and tabletop items. The goods are made in India but with French provincial charm. Absolutely fabulous. There can be a sale in Boston when there isn't one in Nantucket because it's high season, so watch out. Great hostess gifts. Moderate prices; high style.

Hospital Thrift Shop
17 India St., Nantucket

In an old house, on a side street, this used-merchandise mansion offers goodies on a hit-or-miss basis. The smaller stuff is on the first floor; upstairs there is furniture. Stop by on a regular basis to get the benefit of good luck.

Island Trader
Key Post Corner, 35 Old South Rd., Nantucket

Bedding, furniture, wicker. A look, a way of life, a dream.

The Lion's Paw
Zero Main St., Nantucket

Lion's Paw looks like a store straight from the pages of a very classy catalog. Here the decorative items and tableware are newer, brighter, more colorful, more nouveau. Still, elegant and in good taste; one of the best stores in town.

CLAIRE MURRAY
11 S. Water St., Nantucket

We've been collecting used American hooked rugs for many years and thought that perhaps in Nantucket we would splurge and get a kit and make an heirloom. Despite the fact that we are fervent fans of Claire Murray's bright carpets and were prepared to spend a few hundred dollars for this adventure, we lost heart when we discovered a kit costs about $200 and a finished rug about $300. We did happen upon the summer sale when a savings of 20% was offered on a few styles, so that a $455 runner was reduced to $364. Unfortunately, the kit we wanted wasn't on sale. Murray has written a book titled *Nantucket Inspirations,* which is gorgeous and brings home a taste of Nantucket style to those who don't want to go the distance with a carpet. Call 800/252-4733 for the catalog.

NANTUCKET LOOMS
16 Main St., Nantucket

One of the best stores I've ever been to, this store has heart and soul and a lot of great merchandise. It feels good here. The mood is one of elegance and charm, and they could sell you anything. The stock is a collection of their handwoven fabrics (by the yard, in the back of the store), ready-to-wear (from their fabrics), crafts, baskets, hooked rugs, antiques, along with goodies for the home and table.

WEEDS
14 Centre St., Nantucket

Ever want to step inside the pages of a home-decorating magazine like *House Beautiful?* This store, which sells antiques, repro furniture, table arts, and the kind of items you just admire for their style and grace, is filled to brimming with the details that dress up a home or table.

ERICA WILSON
25 Main St., Nantucket

One of the Main Street stores that defines chic, Nantucket style, and New England charm all in one breath. While the store is lovely and divine to explore, it is very pricey. Wilson is famous for her needlepoint—you buy the canvas and wool separately here—and her fine taste; the store also sells gift items and sweaters.

MUSEUM SHOPS

WHALING MUSEUM SHOP
Broad St., Nantucket

Attached to the Whaling Museum is a very fine museum shop with a wide selection of gifts and books. Most items are reproductions of colonial art.

NANTUCKET HISTORICAL ASSOCIATION
1 Broad St., Nantucket

Sells a lightship basket scarf à la Hermès.

SPORTSWEAR

BRAMHALL & DUNN
16 Federal St., Nantucket

There is another branch of this store in Martha's Vineyard that completely bowled us over; this store is smaller but carries the same wonderful stock: expensive sweaters, handbags, hats, and adorable knickknacks. There's kind of a rich hippie feel to the merchandise—the kind of European chic that is the core of the wealthy Island look.

CASHMERE
1 Orange St., Nantucket

The shop of choice for the lady who jet-sets rather than jet-skis.

IRRESISTIBLES
34 Main St., Nantucket

My best buy one summer came from this shop; a cotton summer-cardigan sweater knitted in a bright starfish-and-beach motif—it was on sale for a mere $54. This is the kind of sweater that could pass for a $500 sweater, the kind that is also sold at Irresistibles. This is a branch of a chain with other stores; the stores are good everywhere.

MURRAY'S TOGGERY SHOP
62–68 Main St., Nantucket

MURRAY'S WAREHOUSE
7 New St., Nantucket

Murray's claim to fame is the Nantucket Red washed broadcloth from which they make the clothing that has become the status symbol of Nantucket.

The name and fabric are trademarked, so while you will see similar items around town, there is only one Nantucket Red. Murray's sells clothes for the whole family. They have shoes, all-weather gear, and a lot of Ralph Lauren shirts at high prices. If you forgot to pack enough white or khaki trousers (or Bermudas), fill your wardrobe void here. They now keep great hours: Monday through Saturday, 8:30am to 7pm; Sunday, 10am to 6pm. Murray's Warehouse offers old stock on sale; not much in the way of Reds, however.

NOBBY CLOTHES SHOP
17 Main St., Nantucket

This is Murray's main competition: They have their own version of Nantucket Red called Breton Red. At the risk of being heretics, we will admit we like this store, and this cloth, better. A pair of men's Bermuda shorts in either fabric costs the same (about $35). Nobby sells women's and men's clothing with the usual preppy look.

CARROLL REED
Candle St., Nantucket

If you study your map, you'll see that Candle Street is the southern extension of Water Street as it continues past Main Street. On it, you'll find the Carroll Reed store selling a combination of basic looks and real-world fashion.

JOAN VASS
23 Centre St., Nantucket

One of my favorite designers in life and in sportswear and in casual chic. This store is so tiny that you can miss it. If you are a fan of Joan Vass and her casual, comfortable knit elegance, make sure to seek it out. The knits are basics in either solids or stripes and go easily from one year to the next.

ZERO MAIN
Zero Main St., Nantucket

Good resource for shoes and basics; somewhat hip clothes for teens and youngsters, but still plenty for the prep. Moderately priced, although this look can be found at The Gap for less. Since there is no Gap in Nantucket, however, I suggest Zero Main.

NANTUCKET WOMAN
36 Centre St., Nantucket

Plus-size fashions.

MARTHA'S VINEYARD

Martha's Vineyard is closer to the mainland than Nantucket, larger than Nantucket, and so completely different from Nantucket that it's impossible to know why most people lump them in the same category. Nantucket is like a foreign port; Martha's Vineyard is an American jumble of several resort lifestyles.

Martha's Vineyard is not a huge island, but it is big enough to host three very different, distinct shopping cities. These three cities (Edgartown, Oak Bluffs, and Vineyard Haven) are not far from each other. At opposite ends of the island are Chappaquiddick Island (put on the map by Ted Kennedy) and the "Up-Island" communities like Menemsha (put on the map by Jacqueline Kennedy). Neither of these outer-reaches offers much in terms of shopping, which is why people choose to visit them.

Since Martha's Vineyard is an island, you will either fly in on a small plane or take the ferry. Ferries depart from New Bedford, Woods Hole, and Hyannis and arrive at one of the two port cities on the island: Oak Bluffs or Vineyard Haven (depending on the line you take and your point of departure). If you are on a day trip, without a car, be sure of the city you are going into. You may or may not have choices, based on your departure city.

If you're continuing on to Nantucket from Martha's Vineyard, pay attention to which line you are with because not all ferries offer intraisland service. Once you get to Nantucket, you cannot get back to Woods Hole or New Bedford on the ferry without returning to Martha's Vineyard. Many a tourist has been stranded in the wrong city—and enjoyed a $50 taxicab ride to their desired destination as a result.

You may park your car at the ferry terminal; rates are charged per calendar day, not by a 24-hour period. If you are bringing your car on-island, make sure you have reservations in both directions. The only ferry that takes cars departs from Woods Hole and goes to both port cities on Martha's Vineyard.

If you don't bring the car, you'll need a taxi when you arrive. There are taxi stands at the pier; you simply register. There are several companies, so calling for a ride is no problem. The taxis are vans and will take several passengers. Prices are per group, by destination. (There's a system for this—we just haven't cracked it yet.)

If you're the type who likes to explore, you might want a rental car. Don't be shocked if the rental-car agencies at the pier are jam-packed on summer days—tempers may run high. Big-name rental-car agencies have the best locations by the pier, but also the highest prices.

There are car-rental discounts and promotions available; watch for ads in local publications and mention them at the time you make your reservation. Cars are also available at the airport, in Oak Bluffs, and in Vineyard Haven.

People also rent bikes, mopeds, etc. There's a bus between the three down-island communities. We thought it would be great fun to ride it. It was 100° outside and the bus did not run quite on schedule. We called Budget.

Vineyard Saavy

Martha's Vineyard is often written as MV on T-shirts and sweats; it is never called "MV" when speaking. In conversation, it's "the Vineyard."

Prices are outrageously high. And it's for the same stuff available on the mainland. Prices may be high on Nantucket, but the merchandise there is at least unique. There is little to buy in Martha's Vineyard that can't be found for less off the island.

There is a wonderful handbook to life on Martha's Vineyard called *Guide to Martha's Vineyard,* by Polly Burroughs. You can find it in stores on the Vineyard, at ferry terminals on the mainland, and all around Cape Cod. Although the book costs $12, it does have a fair amount of information in it. There are also free local publications, some with maps.

Martha's Vineyard is much more casual than Nantucket. Much, much, more casual. This is its main attraction to many visitors, in fact. We noted that a few people dressed for dinner, but not that many. Just about anything is acceptable for day wear.

Store Hours & Addresses

Stores open between 9 and 10am, and stay open as late as 10pm in the summer. Sunday is a big day for retail in season. Many stores do not use street numbers, especially if they are on the main street.

Arts & Antiques

There is a percentage of the population devoted to arts, antiques, yard sales, and such pursuits, but they are on the local side. There is not much organized for tourists. You can read the paper to find advertised yard sales (Tuesday and Friday), check out the galleries, or hope there might be a small antiques show in town. There's more to be found in the art/literary world than in the antiques/design world, although you can drive around the island to a handful of antiques shops. Ask around because the good stuff is hidden from tourists. **The Granary Gallery** at **Red Barn Emporium** (Old Country Road, West Tisbury) is one of the hubs of the action. They offer the best selection of antiques and the best insight into what's happening where.

Edgartown

Of the three shopping cities of Martha's Vineyard, Edgartown is regarded by most visitors as the best. (We disagree.) It is certainly the most commercial. It has the most hustle and bustle. It has fabulous architecture. It is a great place to look at. The shopping is—to us—less than enchanting.

If you ask me, Edgartown has two distinct shopping personalities. As we walk down the main street (Lower Main Street), we are reminded of Miami. If we walk on North Water Street, the other main shopping drag, we recall Bermuda. The air of tourism is ripe in this city, and the parting of visitors from their money is so professional, it's hard to define this town as charming. And yet, as you stroll the streets in the evening air, a few shops will beckon you in.

FINDS

PAST AND PRESENTS
37 Lower Main St., Edgartown

A darling store we can't resist, this shop sells the country look in antiques and gifts, as well as more predictable items, like Crabtree & Evelyn products. You'll also find jams, Victorian-style nightgowns, Spode dishes, needlepoint pillows, crockery, steak knives with fish handles, botanical prints—you get the idea. Fair prices.

SUNDOG
41 Lower Main St., Edgartown

Perhaps our favorite store in Edgartown, Sundog sells a "New England sea dog meets Banana Republic" look in rugged all-weather clothes. They have their own T-shirts, which are sort of a local "in" thing; they also sell big canvas tote bags, perfect for that preppy sailing look.

TASHTEGO
Lower Main St., Edgartown

One of the most visually inviting stores, Tashtego sells gift and tabletop items—many of them imports from Mexico and South America. There are Portuguese ceramics and lots of seashell and beach motifs in a variety of designs.

WILSON HOUSE SHOPS
17 N. Water St., Edgartown

Good combination of leather clothes, jeans, some sweaters, and the casual look of rich chic. Many hats, some belts. Good feel to it.

Oak Bluffs

While you stand on the ferry and come into Oak Bluffs, you get a marvelous view of Victorian architecture and a rising sense of anticipation. The town looks great. It continues to look great as you first wander the streets, or as your taxi pulls away toward Edgartown. What adorable little houses! What cute little stores! When you get down to serious shopping, however, you'll find the town has two main parts: a main shopping street (Circuit Avenue) and a cluster of shopping around the ferry pier, which looks good until you realize that it is largely unoccupied. Maybe things will be more lively when you get to town, but Oak Bluffs was pretty depressed when we came around.

The ferry comes to port at a tiny peninsula of land that you may think is downtown. It isn't. You can walk to downtown, but should have your map in hand because even though you only have to cross one street to get there, it's not easy to find the main street.

The main shopping street is called Circuit Avenue. It's lined with tourist shops, fudge parlors, muffin makers, ice-cream shops, and restaurants. There is a grocery store that is smaller than a supermarket, but it has the basics and more. There is a pharmacy, a few stores, and a movie theater.

Finds

CRAFTWORKS
Circuit Ave., Oak Bluffs

Best crafts shop for miles.

THE SECRET GARDEN
Circuit Ave., Oak Bluffs

Crabtree & Evelyn and assorted Victorian-style gifts in the cutest shop in town.

Take It Easy Baby
Circuit Ave., Oak Bluffs

Vintage clothes, surplus, and fashions appealing to those under 20 and not employed by IBM.

Vineyard Haven

Vineyard Haven reminds me of Woodstock, New York, in the good old days of the early 1970s: There's a joyous funkiness to it that celebrates life (and shopping) while still having a lot of class. The town is casual, in a classy way. Almost all the stores are good; true style is for sale. It's an artsy atmosphere, not a beachy one, and there's very little that feels fake or phony.

Vineyard Haven is a village in the town of Tisbury, and if you think that's confusing, wait till you drive into town and can't figure out where you are. When you get to "downtown"—the commercial district on Main Street—you are in Vineyard Haven. Main Street is one-way, and parking around town is hard to find. There are only one or two little side streets to prowl. This is really a one-street town.

Finds

Augusta
Main St., Vineyard Haven

Santa Fe–look that works amazingly well in New England. A fabulous store with gifts, pottery, twig furniture, rugs, Southwestern style, and more. Some Mexican glass.

The Balcony
Main St., Vineyard Haven

This is a crafts shop that did not impress us tremendously, but we saw one item that was magnificent and that's all it takes. So, stop by and get lucky.

BRAMHALL & DUNN
Main St., Vineyard Haven

This is the best store in town and one of the best stores we've ever seen, simply because it is bought so precisely it makes you want to be the kind of person who buys these things, who looks like this. There are expensive hand-knit sweaters, designer hats, and little flat shoes made in China and finished with ribbons and flowers. Housewares and bed linens are upstairs.

CHILMARK POTTERY
Main St., Vineyard Haven

The pottery part of the store is on one side, a leather shop makes up the rest of the store. The pottery is a nice earthenware with a colonial touch, or maybe a country touch. In any case, it works in a modern world. A gorgeous pitcher at $65 seems fairly priced.

MURRAY'S OF THE VINEYARD
Main St., Vineyard Haven

This isn't one of the best stores in town, but Murray's is so famous in Nantucket that we want you to know: Yes, this is a branch of the Nantucket store; yes, they sell Nantucket Reds here too. Also women's clothing, Polo/Ralph Lauren, shoes, etc.

RAINY DAY
Main St., Vineyard Haven

A type of general store with housewares and umbrellas and stuff for the kids, and wrapping papers and rugs from India, and teapots and beach goodies, and all the bright colorful things you want to see when you go shopping.

TRAVIS TUCK
89 Main St., Vineyard Haven

The original weathervanes of the gods. Prices begin well over $2,000. Just thought you should know.

Chapter Ten

· · · · · · ·

VERMONT

WELCOME TO VERMONT

· ·

As much as Vermont is like New Hampshire—they can be quite literally two peas in a pod—Vermont is so totally different from New Hampshire that we have to send you to both and let you test the air. These states are neighbors, but they feel miles apart—and one of the main reasons has to do with the shopping.

Even though I've been critical of southern New Hampshire for its commercialization and attempts to integrate into the yuppie Boston hub, I continue to gush over the commercial possibilities in Vermont. It's all got to do with the presentation. Or maybe the cows . . . and the ice cream.

Vermont, more than any other New England state, wants you to associate it with the stereotypical New England fantasy—rolling meadows dotted with black-and-white cows; the ski resorts, as whimsical and dramatic as any in Europe; and the scenic covered bridges, crafts villages, and antiques emporiums. Vermont considers itself a national treasure, an endangered species. The last of the Mohicans, or something like that.

And I have to admit, I totally buy into that fantasy. And I do mean *buy*. So come on up to Vermont. And bring your credit cards.

GETTING THERE

. . . .

Burlington is the major transportation center of Vermont with an airport; the Amtrak station in Burlington has been replaced by a station stop at Essex Junction, 2 miles away.

A car is essential for getting around the state, though most resorts and ski communities have shuttle service from train stations and airports. You can rent wheels upon arrival. Amtrak offers sleeper service with old-fashioned sleeper cars, but the price tag is incredibly steep and may rival plane fare. (Two round-trip tickets from Stamford, CT, to Waterbury, VT: $400!)

BURLINGTON

. . . .

Burlington is headquarters for "real-people" shopping; this is where the locals go when they want to do some serious shopping and actually get what they need from a bigger-than-country-store selection. Tourists will prefer out-of-town shopping because they want the sights and sounds of Vermont, but Burlington has a few things worth mentioning besides the local mall.

Finds

CHAMPLAIN MILL
1 Main St., Winooski

This restored mill is on the Winooski River near Lake Champlain and has three floors of shops and eats. About 2 miles north of town; take Exit 16 off I-89.

CHURCH STREET MARKETPLACE
Church St., Burlington

Downtown Burlington's alternative to the mall. One hundred shops in an enclosed marketplace with a festival-like air. Street vendors add to the fun.

JELLY MILL COMMON
Rte. 7, south of Burlington

Overly cute New England village–style retail for tourists. There's another like it in Manchester. OK for a quick browse or lunch.

SHELBURNE MUSEUM
Rte. 7, Shelburne

If you are interested in decorative arts, then you had better plan your visit to the Shelburne Museum right now, as this is perhaps the leading museum of folk art. The museum is made up of the Tuckaway General Store (a cafeteria and museum dedicated to 19th-century retail) and the Museum and Country stores. Prices are less expensive at the Country Store. Shelburne is just south of Burlington and is near Burlington International Airport. The museum is open daily, but on a seasonal basis. Call 802/985-3344 to see if they'll be open when you visit.

MIDDLEBURY

. . . .

Welcome to the heart of Vermont and a typical little hamlet (fewer than 10,000 residents). Home to Middlebury College, the famous Middlebury Writer's Conference, and lots of little places to shop and enjoy. From mansions to museums to crafts centers and country stores, it's all here.

Finds

FACTORY MARKETPLACE AT KENNEDY BROTHERS
11 Main St., Vergennes

One hundred fifty stores in a giant brick creamery featuring many local craft artisans. Play area for the kids. Vergennes is between Shelburne and Middlebury.

HOLY COW
52 Seymour St., Middlebury

Holy Cow is right! Those Holsteins may just look like cows to you, but by the time you've been in New England for a few hours, you'll begin to see them as regional landmarks. After you've seen Woody Jackson's work, on sale here, you'll consider them shrines. Jackson is the artist who has made black-and-white cows famous. Other cows may be clichés; Jackson's are art. Call for a catalog (☎ 800/543-COWS—of course), or stop by the store. This address is not in downtown Middlebury, so ask directions in town. It's not totally in the boonies either; there are other shopping opportunities like **Danforth Pewters** (next door) and the nearby **Marble Works** (a rehab full of cute stores). It's worth the drive, but if you miss it, prices in the catalog include paid postage. And hey, where else are you going to find a cow yo-yo for $4?

MIDDLEBURY ANTIQUES CENTER
East Middlebury

Fifty dealers specializing in country looks and Americana, located at the junction of Route 7 and Route 116.

VERMONT STATE CRAFT CENTER
Mill St., Frog Hollow, Middlebury

Crafts gallery featuring 250 different craftspeople, located right in the Frog Hollow District. Open

Sunday only during season. See page 91 for more on the local crafts scene. Also check out **Sweet Cecily** on Frog Hollow Lane for more crafts.

BENNINGTON

. . . .

There are two main streets in Bennington: Route 7 and Main Street (Route 9). The town is divided into quadrants from where they intersect. To the west (on Route 9) is the Bennington Battle Monument and the part of town called Old Bennington. If you drive past the monument toward North Bennington (and Bennington College), you'll pass several covered bridges and a railroad station that's been converted into a restaurant. Most of the fun shopping is not on the main shopping streets, so be prepared to drive around and spend some time exploring.

There are also a few outlets in town; perhaps more will gather together.

Finds

BENNINGTON MUSEUM
West Main St. (Rte. 9), Bennington

Good, small museum of Americana featuring Grandma Moses and tons of Bennington pottery, which has been made here for over 150 years. Naturally, there's the **Museum Shop** for Vermont-made specialties and Grandma Moses postcards. There is also a good genealogy library here. During January and February, the museum is only open on weekends. In July, the museum usually sponsors an antiques show.

BENNINGTON POTTERS' YARD
324 Country St., Bennington

You've heard of the famous Bennington pottery, maybe even seen it at the museum; now's your chance to buy. Also glassware and even a great place to eat. This site combines the best elements of a great store, a tourist attraction, and a factory outlet, resulting in a spree to remember.

CB FACTORY OUTLET
190 North St. (Rte. 7), Bennington

You don't have to wait for Manchester for the factory outlets. Bennington has a few of its own. The CB Outlet will be popular with the status conscious in your family. We hit a sale and winter jackets were $29.99. Adults' and children's sizes.

VERMONT WOODEN PLAYTHINGS
Overlea Rd., Bennington

Great quality at somewhat high prices, but these are the toys that get handed down through families, and may well be collectible. These wooden toys look like craft pieces, but are made to withstand the rigors of childhood games and will last well into the next generation.

MANCHESTER

. . . .

OK, so Manchester means factory outlets to most of America, and to us, too, but we do want you to know that Manchester Center also boasts some nice architecture and culture, and the rural area offers things to look at besides bargains. The town has indeed been taken over by outlets, the crowds can be fierce, and the traffic will snarl. But the shopping can give you a real high, and the city is one of the classiest of all of the outlet towns.

In fact, after shopping almost every outlet in New England, I think Manchester offers some of the best experiences. You can combine New England charm and scenery with a good hotel for the family, some romance (if you want), many ice-cream cones (don't miss Ben & Jerry's!) and some serious credit-card flipping. There are a number of high-end designer shops in Manchester, so the crowd is upscale and the bargains are real.

If you are coming from a foreign country and looking for one outlet city, this one is perhaps the best. It's just not quite as crowded as Freeport and it's much more charming than Kittery.

The Lay of the Land

There's Manchester Center, and there's Manchester Village, and they aren't the same place, although neither is inconvenient to the other. If you are looking for a place to sleep, the really good places are in Manchester Village. Driving on Route 7, exit at Route 30, which is marked as "Manchester Depot." Follow Route 30 into town and you'll begin to see freestanding outlets. This is one of the times it pays to drive the whole area before stopping to shop. There are tons of outlets and you may want to be selective.

Follow Route 30 until it comes to a fork. Route 7A is to the left; Route 30 continues to the right. There's more shopping in both directions, but if you take Route 7A to the left, you'll hit Manchester Village and several nice inns and eateries. And more outlet stores.

If you prefer a more scenic route, and aren't in a hurry to get to those bargains, take Route 7A right after Bennington and follow it north to Manchester Village. You'll pass through Shaftsbury and Arlington, both nice for browsing. You'll also go by Hildene, the lavish summer home once owned by Robert Todd Lincoln.

The best outlet malls are congregated in a downtown core where Route 30 and Route 7A meet. They are **Manchester Commons** and **Battenkill Plaza.** All other freestanding outlets come and go. The town is continuing to take on new tenants, so change is constant.

Manchester Commons is a large mall, divided into parts, so addresses can get confusing. There is an enclosed mall portion, with stores indoors, and then a chain of attached stores that front Route 30 and look like old-fashioned Main Street shops.

Do take the time to sit down with some of the free literature provided around town in the stores and hotels. Bear in mind that maps and lists may go out of date quickly.

Factory Outlets

For a complete description, see the section on factory-outlet stores in the front part of this book. To whet your shopping appetite, here's a list of some of the most upscale outlet stores available: **Boston Traders/Traders Kids; Brooks Brothers; Donna Karan; Anne Klein; Calvin Klein Company Store; Arlene La Marca; Coach; Polo/Ralph Lauren; Movado/Wings; Orvis; and Cole-Haan.**

Explore on your own. There's something here for everyone—and usually it's half its original retail price!

ARLINGTON

. . . .

When you think you are going to crack from the intensity of the outlet shopping in Manchester and the vicinity, and you need to remind yourself that you did come to see New England, we recommend that you hit Route 7A. Drive around, poke through the shops, and smell the fresh country air.

Actually, Arlington and East Arlington and Shaftsbury are back on the road toward Bennington, so you may want to hit these villages on the way to Manchester. If you're using Manchester as a base for your skiing or shopping trip, it's easy enough to backtrack.

Finds

ARLINGTON GALLERY
Rte. 7A, Arlington

Norman Rockwell gallery where many of the guides were also models of his. Naturally, there's a gift shop.

CANDLE MILL VILLAGE
Old Mill Rd., East Arlington

Some toy shops and other tiny stores in this "mill village." Also candle-dipping, which your kids should adore.

EAST ARLINGTON ANTIQUES CENTER
Old Mill Rd., East Arlington

Don't say you should drive here just for this one store, but while you're in town anyway, take a peek at this funky antiques center that sprawls through the upstairs of an old house. Different dealers set up their own areas. Prices are moderate.

HAGELBERG FARM MAPLE PRODUCTS
Rte. 7A, Arlington

A sugaring operation just south of Arlington where you can take in a free exhibit on making maple syrup and take home the house brand. Open all year.

SUNDERLAND COUNTRY SHOPPES
Rte. 7A, Arlington

Directly across from Basketville, this touristy country store is actually rather fun. They have everything from local specialties to your basic souvenirs.

STRATTON

. . . .

I do not ski. I shop. Although we went to Stratton to take a look and try it, we found the environment so foreign that all we could do was go shopping and race down the hill back to Manchester and the bargains.

Friends who do ski say there are unbelievable bargains to be had at end-of-season sales in all the stores, at all the resorts. We checked out a number of places at the outdoor mall in Stratton (**The Shops At Village Square**) and found a number of good shops, but prices were sky high.

Stratton Sports can outfit you—and any member of the family, in hip slope style—as long as price is no object. The same is true at **Bogner** and **CB Sports**. Kids' wear at **Yellow Turtle** is adorable. And both **Gallery North Star** and **Handworks** are excellent crafts galleries. There are about 20 shops in the mall altogether, and a bank for getting more cash— which you will surely need if you are shopping here.

Note: Parking is impossible. If you're here just to shop, you may want to think twice.

SMUGGLER'S NOTCH & STOWE

When I confessed to a friend that Stratton was not our cup of tea, and perhaps we would never be ski bunnies, she just laughed. "Try Smuggler's Notch," she said, "and then go shopping in Stowe." Thank you, Candyce.

Smuggler's Notch is a real family kind of place; it's in a private world created by Mother Nature and the Smuggler's Notch Corporation and offers a year-round vacation center (with shopping, of course) and proximity to Stowe so you can take in the big-time and money without spending too much of your own. Between these two communities, you'll find the best of Vermont's resort-shopping possibilities.

If you book a Smuggler's Notch package, you get special airfare deals with USAir that bring you into Burlington, about 30 miles away. We went by train, alighting in Waterbury so we could rent a car, drive around the countryside, and take in the **Ben & Jerry** ice-cream factory. Smuggler's Notch does offer a shuttle from the train station at Essex Junction. Car rentals can also be arranged by Smuggler's.

With Smuggler's kids programs, you can leave your children on the slopes or in another program and go off to shop or explore on your own. There is also day care for children up to 6 years old.

If you are traveling north to Jeffersonville (home of Smuggler's Notch) from Waterbury, you can have a shopping spree along Route 100, where you'll pass through Waterbury and Stowe. There are a variety of antiques shops scattered along Route 100. When you hit Route 15, you'll turn left and head for Johnson and then down into Jeffersonville, where Smuggler's is. You can than continue south past Mount Mansfield and back to Stowe on Route 108 (which is also dotted with antiques shops).

Finds

BEN & JERRY FACTORY
Rte. 100, Waterbury

So it's really not a factory outlet, but this is the state's biggest tourist attraction and you do get a free sample of the product (how many factories can say that?). This is Vermont's most famous ice cream. The tour is offered year-round, though factory hours vary with the season. The admission fee goes to support environmental causes.

BREWSTER RIVER MILL
Mill St. (Rte. 108), Jeffersonville

Picture-book–perfect grist mill with a steam engine, rehabbed to house retail shops specializing in local foods and products. Closed in winter.

COLD HOLLOW CIDER MILL
Rte. 100, Waterbury Center

They press cider all year, so you don't have to worry if you don't get here in the autumn. The mill store sells local foodstuffs and many apple products. They have a mail-order program. This is the kind of place that takes full advantage of how wonderful their product is. Hours are generally 10am to 6pm; they're open until 7pm during foliage season. They have a toll-free number: ☎ 800/3-APPLES in the U.S., or 800/UC-CIDER in Vermont.

EVERYTHING COWS
Main St., Stowe

Udderly wonderful . . . a wide range of cow products, arts, decorative touches, gag gifts, and even a cowtalog.

JOHNSON WOOLEN MILL FACTORY STORE
Rte. 15, Johnson

Sort of a local hero, known for its traditional woolens and hunting clothes since 1842. Clothing for all members of the family, as well as hats, mittens, vests, and blankets. Vermont products and foodstuffs are also sold. There is a seconds room. They have Sunday hours in winter from September through Christmas; Saturday from 9am to 4pm; weekdays from 8am to 5pm.

THE OLD DEPOT SHOPS
Main St., Stowe

Several boutiques located at the corner of Main and Depot streets in a rehab known as The Depot Building by locals. Winners here include The Craft Sampler, Bear Pond Books, Pure Vermont Artistry, and Stuffed in Stowe, which is a shop featuring stuffed bears.

SMUGGLERS CREATIONS
Mountain Rd. (Rte. 108), Jeffersonville

This shop sells new quilts designed to become heirlooms; they have several hundred designs available. Custom work is also available.

Smuggler's Forge Craft Gallery
Mountain Rd. (Rte. 108), Jeffersonville

Crafts and antiques in an atmosphere of mountain coziness. Open June through October only.

Stowe Antiques Center
Masonic Bldg., Main St., Stowe

Multidealer venue right on the main street of town for fun browsing and country goodies.

Stowe Pottery
Mountain Rd., Stowe

Get out the camera! Get out the money! Take a photo of that covered bridge. Look at the studio. Then after the scenery sinks in, latch on to some earthenware pottery.

Vermont Rug Makers
Rte. 100C, East Johnson

The weavers are right here and will happily explain their art to you. Choose from rugs of various sizes; they will take a custom order. Closed on Sunday, but open year-round otherwise.

Waterbury Flea Market
Rte. 2, Waterbury

What could be better than an outdoor flea market in Vermont? Held on Saturday and Sunday and holidays, as weather permits, from about the second week in May through October.

Chapter Eleven

· · · · · · · ·

NEW HAMPSHIRE & SOUTHERN MAINE

COASTING ALONG

· ·

The coastal sweep of Route 1 through northern Massachusetts, New Hampshire, and into southern Maine is one of our favorite New England adventures. Along this route you'll find everything you dream about when you think New England: seaports, colonial architecture, lobsters, beaches, and factory outlets.

PORTSMOUTH

· ·

Some people consider Portsmouth to be one of Boston's more distant suburbs. The commute is only an hour, yet you reap all of the New Hampshire benefits—no sales tax, no state income tax, and proximity to **Kittery** and **North Conway**. Of course, this is all from a shopping perspective. Portsmouth is also a beautiful colonial village with a living-history museum called **Strawberry Banke.** There's a lot to see and do here and a fair amount of retail mixed in among the natural charm. And the location couldn't be better.

Located right on the water, just off I-95, Portsmouth is the perfect place to park yourself in order to explore northern Massachusetts, southern New Hampshire, and lower Maine. And of course, you can easily swing down to Boston.

Exit 7 off of I-95 leads you right into downtown Portsmouth and onto Market Street, the main drag. This is where you'll find the Chamber of Commerce and their guide to the area called *Guide to the Seacoast*. This free booklet is full of maps and shop listings. There are even coupons good for discounts at area shops and services. Right outside of town is Newington, close enough for us to consider it part of Portsmouth. This is where the malls are located.

To explore downtown Portsmouth, we suggest the "aimless wandering" approach. Peek down alleys and around the corners of the colonial homes; you'll see stores everywhere in the bustling downtown area. On State Street, there's an antiques area.

Finds

COUNTRY CURTAINS
2299 Woodbury Ave., Portsmouth

A little way out of town and on the way to North Conway, this curtain resource is located in a wonderful old house: The Old Beane Farm. Follow Market Street until it becomes Woodbury Avenue, pass the malls, and the store is on your right.

GALLERY 33
Market St., Portsmouth

Very fine crafts shop specializing in whimsical ceramics and pottery. Some work in other mediums is also represented.

MACRO POLO
89 Market St., Portsmouth

North Hampton Factory Outlet Center

North Hampton is actually south of Portsmouth. This is not one of the more famous outlet centers, and we prefer Kittery, but if you want to avoid paying sales tax or are sticking to the southern part of the coastal area, here's your chance to hit about 35 outlet stores including **Timberland, American Tourister,** and **Bass Shoe** (see Chapter 4 for more). They're all along Route 1, in North Hampton, New Hampshire.

I want to call this shop Marco Polo, since you'll feel like an explorer as you wander into this small den crammed with silly gifts, toys, magic tricks, gag items, and oddities. Your kids will never want to leave.

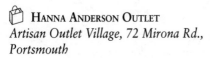 HANNA ANDERSON OUTLET
Artisan Outlet Village, 72 Mirona Rd.,
Portsmouth

Outlet store for adorable cotton baby clothes sold from the Hanna Anderson catalog. Worth a special trip. Open daily.

STRAWBERRY BANKE MUSEUM STORE/
THE DUNAWAY STORE
Marcy St., Portsmouth

Strawberry Banke is a living-history museum, which means when you enter the park grounds, you take a step back in history. This 10-acre museum has 42 properties dating back to 1630. At the edge of it all, across from a magnificent floral garden, is the museum shop. This little wooden house is chock-full of reproduction gifts and goodies.

NORTH CONWAY

. . . .

I first discovered North Conway almost by accident. Aaron went to camp nearby. Parents were sent to a motel in North Conway. If you can imagine, at that time we actually had no idea it was one of the nation's factory-outlet capitals. Well, we caught on fast.

North Conway has two seemingly different identities: It is the cradle of the White Mountains and a ski/nature resort, and it is a shopping mecca for millions. So you can come to North Conway for the slopes or the shops. Remember, there's no sales tax in New Hampshire, so although many of these stores are also in other locations, this may be the place to make big purchases.

North Conway is a one-street town, and while there is sort of a downtown area (North Conway Village), it is past the concentration of the factory outlets, so if you don't go into town to shop, you may simply miss it.

Almost all the outlets are freestanding. There are a few strip centers (the **L. L. Bean Complex** is excellent), but you will spend a fair amount of time getting in and out of your car and driving to the different outlets. **Settler's Green,** in front of the Sheraton, has a grand selection of shops in an easy-to-get-to shopping mall; parking is convenient.

Finds

L. L. BEAN COMPLEX
Rte. 16, North Conway

This L-shaped strip center is not big, but it is grand: Some of the best names in retail have their outlet stores here. Fans of high-end merchandise and fans of L. L. Bean should make this their first stop. The **L. L. Bean** outlet store is large (two levels); the

Cole-Haan Company Store is also two levels, and very fancy. There is a **Fanny Farmer** outlet store here. **Anne Klein** was not nearly as good as the Maine outlets (selection-wise), but we have done very well at **Ellen Tracy.** Open daily.

MT. WASHINGTON FACTORY OUTLET CENTER
Rte. 16, North Conway

There is a third mini-mall outlet in town, which also carries a lot of high-end merchandise. The location is convenient to the other outlets, so you can leave the car in one of the parking lots and walk here. Tenants include **Chuck Roast, Timberland, Le Sportsac,** and **London Fog.**

POLO/RALPH LAUREN
Rte. 16, North Conway

Good old Ralph has been seriously involved in the factory-outlet business for years; I'm sure you've been to, or at least heard about, his classy outlet stores before. Suffice to say the outlet in North Conway is large, lovely, and very much like all the other Polo outlets around the country.

It is a freestanding store, next door to Calvin Klein and across the street from the L. L. Bean Complex. Since we believe if you've seen one Ralph Lauren outlet, you've seen them all, we're going to tell you about something we found much more interesting: The tent sale held in the parking lot.

This four-day event was so well organized you were given a sheet of paper listing the rules of the sale. Our paper said "Final Sale. No Returns. No Exchanges. No Credits. All Shoes $35. All Belts $10. All Cotton Sweaters $20. All Children's Clothing $10. All Knit Shirts $15."

I've left off some of the listings, but you get the idea. Was it mobbed in the tent? Was there a gorgeous man changing in the bushes while his wife handed clothes over the hedge? Were there women

---

Crafts Too

LEAGUE OF NEW HAMPSHIRE CRAFTSMEN
Rte. 16, North Conway

Since man does not live by outlets alone, you will
be pleased to find this crafts gallery (one of several
by this name scattered around New Hampshire),
where prices are not discounted but the workmanship is unique. Toward the north end of town.

---

grabbing up armloads of shirts; men fighting over
sizes? Was this the most fun I had since Bloomingdale's in Stamford went out of business???

Fill out the guest book; get on the mailing list
and they let you know about future events and all
promotional sales, of which there are many.

REEBOK FACTORY STORE
Rte. 16, North Conway

First off, it's one of the first outlets you come to. It's
freestanding, and if you haven't gotten the hang of
zipping in and out of the parking lots to get to these
stores, you may miss it. This is not the best Reebok
outlet we've ever been to, but it'll do. Aaron has
moved on to Nike, which is elsewhere, but if your
kids wear Reebok, or Weebok, now's your chance
to save.

SETTLER'S GREEN
Rte. 16, North Conway

If you aren't headed right to the L. L. Bean Complex, then this should be your first stop. It's off to
your right before you get to L. L. Bean, and for
some reason is not very well marked. Watch for signs
to the Sheraton. They call themselves an OVP—
Outlet Village Plus. Stores include: **Eddie Bauer,**

J. Crew, Banana Republic, Bugle Boy, Geoffrey Beene, Brookstone, etc.

CANTERBURY

. . . .

There were so few signs to the Shaker Village that we thought our pilgrimage to Canterbury would be a bust. If you're heading south from North Conway toward Concord, you can take Exit 18 from I-93 and follow signs to the Shaker Village in Canterbury, which has some fine shopping opportunities (of course).

We have not been to many of the Shaker communities in New England, so this was our big visit and we enjoyed it tremendously. Canterbury often hosts antiques fairs right on its grounds, which can add to the pleasures of the day. You pay your admission on the main road, then wander through the gates around the farm. The main store is inside the gates, but if you just want to shop without visiting the grounds, say so at the main gate.

There are 22 buildings in the complex; workshops include basket weaving, broom making, chair listing, box making, rug braiding, and spinning and weaving. The main store sells examples of all these crafts. Call 603/783-9511 for workshop details.

KITTERY

. . . .

Never considered Kittery a vacation hot spot? Although there isn't a lot of town here, and there are no colonial relics, we're happy to frolic at the factory outlets. Kittery is the first coastal city in Maine; just a bridge crossing (and a $1 toll) from Portsmouth, New Hampshire; just an hour or so from Boston. (*Note:* In Boston everyone says Kittery is an hour away; it took me 1 hour and 20 minutes.)

You really don't even need the real city of Kittery. What you want is a stretch of Route 1 (Exit 3 off of

Kittery, Maine Outlets

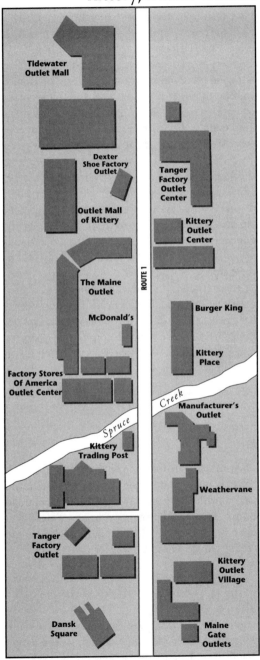

I-95, then follow signs to Coastal Route 1). This two-lane road is lined with strip centers. These strip centers are jammed with factory-outlet shops.

There are very few freestanding outlets, but there is a good bit of moving the car because you cannot walk from center to center. There are outlet malls on both sides of the street. Start on one side, work it until it ends, then turn around and start down the other side. You brought an extra suitcase, right?

Warning: The sheer number of outlet malls is shocking to those who have never seen this scene. Don't be overwhelmed. There is no reason to go to every store. Go to your favorites or high-end, big-name dealers. Be sure to check our directory of outlets (see Chapter 4) to get a better understanding of what's in town and what is actually sold in these stores.

Also, note that crowds can be fierce and finding a parking space can be nerve-racking. Most outlets have benches outside for less enthusiastic shoppers. Bookstores—there's usually one in each strip—may keep nonserious shoppers occupied while you stock up.

Finds

KITTERY OUTLET MALL
Rte. 1, Kittery

This is always my first stop on this side of the road, heading away from Boston. It's modern, fresh, and packed with good stores. Outlets include: **Crate and Barrel, Etienne Aigner, J. Crew,** and **Polo/Ralph Lauren.** You may find this mall listed as **Kittery Outlet Village** on some of the local literature.

KITTERY PLACE
Rte. 1, Kittery

This mall is recognizable by its gold-trimmed-with-white paint job and white columns. You'll find **Nautica, Izod,** and **Puma,** among others.

THE MAINE OUTLET
Rte. 1, Kittery

This is a very large, L-shaped strip center with few kids' stores, a bank machine, a place for a snack and the local McDonald's in the front parking lot. Not every shop in this mall is great, and you can wear yourself out just discovering that fact. You may want to pick and choose. Best bets: **Joan and David**, **Timberland**, and **Mikasa**.

TANGER OUTLET CENTER
Rte. 1, Kittery

Tanger is a big name in town. Their other location is also good. This small L-shaped strip center is anchored by **Brooks Brothers**. Other stores include **Calvin Klein, Adrienne Vittadini, Maidenform, Eagle's Eye,** and more.

TANGER OUTLET CENTER 2
Rte. 1, Kittery

This is a deep strip that heads away from the road. You'll recognize it by the blue roof and nautical motif. If you have menfolk in the family who've been complaining about this trip, this could be their reward stop. Here is where you'll find the two-level **Black & Decker** outlet store. We almost needed a second van for the goodies Mike and Aaron found here. There's also a good selection of stores, including **Anne Klein, Oshkosh, L'eggs, Bass, Liz Claiborne, Carter's Childrenswear,** and **American Tourister.**

TIDEWATER MALL
Rte. 1, Kittery

Looks a bit like a colonial village with a large yellow neoclassical Greek Revival home for the **Lenox** outlet, then a row of other stores including a large **Tapemeasure, Hickey-Freeman, Reed & Barton,** and **Boston Trader** stores.

PORTLAND

If your child goes to camp in Maine, you are probably familiar with Portland—with its airport, car rentals, and Old Port shopping. If not, you should know that Portland is only 2 hours from Boston, and its airport makes it a transportation hub for visitors to and from the state. It's a large city with all the conveniences; tourists will most likely want to explore the scenic part of town by the waterfront, called Old Port.

Finds

THOMAS MOSER
415 Cumberland Ave., Portland

The showroom for this fantastic handcrafted furniture is housed in a restored mansion. Call 207/774-3791 for directions.

LITTLE NEMO'S WORLD OF BOOKS
420 Fore St., Old Port, Portland

Quality old books, maps, prints, and a big fat sleeping pussycat. Open daily.

BLUEBERRIES + GRANITE
422 Fore St., Old Port, Portland

The two ingredients for which Maine is most famous form the name of this store, which sells state-oriented souvenirs that are exactly what you are looking for. Just a few are kitschy, most are fun.

COMMUNIQUES
Corner of Moulton and Commercial sts., Old Port, Portland

Everyone in our family agrees that this is the best store in Old Port. It sells tons of little, silly gifts. If you've got kids in camp, this is a perfect place to stock up for the care packages.

CONCEITS
7 Moulton St., Old Port, Portland

This small jewelry shop sells contemporary, ethnic, and antique jewelry as well as some costume period pieces. Really worth a look.

MAXWELLS
5 Moulton St., Old Port, Portland

Local pottery, earthenware (including works by Monroe Salt Works), some housewares, and nice things for the table.

FREEPORT

. . . .

Freeport. The very mention of it sends shudders up the spine. Shivers through the handbag. The credit cards begin to twitch. Even Grandpa Sy, the world's least enthusiastic shopper, rises to the occasion. "Are we ready for L. L. Bean yet?" Almost, Sy, almost.

The main street of Freeport has been turned into one giant factory mall. Many of the stores are free-standing; there are some strip centers. Everywhere you look there are little houses that have been turned into stores. There are also some important side streets, so study your map. Do not be fooled into thinking all the good stuff is on Main Street. That Anne Klein outlet is very well hidden. The L. L. Bean outlet is a little bit hidden.

And speaking of hidden, all the good stuff isn't only downtown. There's a flea market on weekends (weather permitting) out toward Exit 19 off of I-95, as well as another fairly large outlet mall. Both are located on Route 1, before the visitor's kiosk.

A note about hours: This is a town that never sleeps—it shops. Stores are always open. The

L. L. Bean outlet is open 24 hours a day, every day of the year. Other stores are merely open 7 days a week and close sometime at night, depending on the amount of tourist traffic. (There are extended evening hours in summer and autumn.) Stores open at 9am (10am on Sunday) and close around 6 or 7pm, except when they are on late-night hours, which means they close around 9pm. Sunday hours are until 6 or 7pm, depending on the time of year.

A note about crowds: This town is mobbed, absolutely mobbed. Parking can be scarce; tempers can flare. You may have to stand in line to go to the bathroom or to get an ice cream. Don't bring the kids. Don't bring the infirm. Don't bring your husband (if you can help it).

Please note that not all of these stores are outlets! You can make some expensive mistakes if you don't look before you leap. Some are retail stores, some are worse. We think the Gap outlet is a joke; this is markdown merchandise at the exact same prices as at your local Gap without any benefit of selection or charm. **Cole-Haan** has discounted merchandise downstairs only, and **Nike** has it upstairs. Let the buyer beware!

Finds

THE COACH FACTORY STORE
48 West St., Freeport

We point this out because it is rather on its own at the far end of Main Street and not in the thick of things. Like all Coach outlet stores, this one is a winner. The entrance is on West Street, but you can see it from Main Street—it's really on the corner.

DOONEY & BOURKE FACTORY STORE
52 Main St., Freeport

This is good news and bad news all wrapped up together. Since there aren't a lot of Dooney & Bourke outlet stores in New England, we go to lengths to point you to this one, which is behind and downstairs in a mall center on Main Street. Prices are certainly less than in your local department store. But prices can be better in Norwalk, Connecticut (see page 44), if you just happen to be going there. Otherwise, now's your chance to buy a real New England status symbol. Prices begin around $99 for a handbag.

L. L. BEAN
Main St., Freeport

We're making the wild assumption that you know all about L. L. Bean and don't need a normal listing here. So we're going to tell you the esoteric consumer bits and pieces we know might be refreshingly new. So here goes, in no particular order:

- Call 800/221-4221, 24 hours a day, 7 days a week, every day of the year for information about your shopping needs, including stock and availability. They have very nice operators. There is TDD for deaf customers: Call 800/545-0090.
- Do not confuse the main store with the outlet store, which is called the factory store, in Freeport. There are three factory stores currently. There may be sales in the main store, but the serious markdowns are in another building.
- If you are an old-time customer of either store or catalog, please note that shipping is no longer included in the price of an item; you pay a one-time (per address) shipping charge of $4.50 from either store or catalog. If you are making several purchases from various parts of the store (main store only), you can collect your packages and take them to the packing desk (expect to stand in line), where these items will be shipped to you for the flat fee of $4.50, no matter how much they weigh.

- If you do not already receive the mail-order catalog, you may sign up for the mailing list in the entryway on the first-floor level. There is a small atrium here as you enter; look slightly to your left and you'll see a give-away area that has free folders with how-to information, much conservation literature, and forms for the catalog. You may also get a free catalog while you are in the store. Please note that aside from the "general" catalogs, there are specialty catalogs. Special interests include: fly fishing, winter sports, spring sports, hunting, home and camp, and women's wear. There are two different sign-up forms: general and specialty.

- It is smart (if you have the stamina) to browse the regular retail store first, honing in on those areas of interest you are planning to conquer. Do not buy anything. Mosey over to the factory store, see what's here, what the discount is (as merchandise may be similar, but not exactly the same), where you can save money, and where you can't compromise. After making purchases in the factory store, return to the mother ship, wave your credit cards and shop, shop, shop.

L. L. BEAN FACTORY STORE
Depot St., Freeport

The factory store sells mostly clothing and footgear, although there are some knives in a counter at the cash register, and there is an area of odds and ends that have been discontinued or haven't sold for whatever reasons. This is where you may score on a tent or a mailbox. Two items of interest:

They are human; they make mistakes on tickets. We saw a down vest in the outlet store in North Conway for $30; the same vest (but now in the right size) was marked for $45 in the factory store in Freeport. We asked for a computer price check and were rewarded with the information that yes, indeedy, the correct price was $30.

The tags are color-coded; the code is explained on posters around the store—which you may have ignored in your haste to shop. The color code determines what additional discount you get at the cash register. So the $30 vest was marked down an additional 20%. Markdowns by code may be as high as 50% of the lowest ticketed price.

THE NIKE STORE
11 Bow St., Freeport

This is state-of-the-art retail, and even though it's not an outlet (some discounts upstairs), the displays, the TV sets, and the video action are something you've gotta see.

YANKEE CANDLE COMPANY
6 Mill St., Freeport

So you brought the kids anyway—we told you not to—and they've seen L. L. Bean, and you've bought ice cream all around and now, before you kill them, quick, head to the candle store. You cannot dip candles here (it's against fire regulations), the shop is small, there are no seconds (everything here is regular retail price), but the kids seem to love all the colors. Open daily, 10am to 8pm.

Size Conversion Chart

. . . .

Women's Dresses, Coats and Skirts

American	3	5	7	9	11	12	13	14	15	16	18
Continental	36	38	38	40	40	42	42	44	44	46	48
British	8	10	11	12	13	14	15	16	17	18	20

Women's Blouses and Sweaters

American	10	12	14	16	18	20
Continental	38	40	42	44	46	48
British	32	34	36	38	40	42

Women's Shoes

American	5	6	7	8	9	10
Continental	36	37	38	39	40	41
British	$3^1/_2$	$4^1/_2$	$5^1/_2$	$6^1/_2$	$7^1/_2$	$8^1/_2$

Children's Clothing

American	3	4	5	6	6X
Continental	98	104	110	116	122
British	18	20	22	24	26

Children's Shoes

American	8	9	10	11	12	13	1	2	3
Continental	24	25	27	28	29	30	32	33	34
British	7	8	9	10	11	12	13	1	2

Men's Suits

American	34	36	38	40	42	44	46	48
Continental	44	46	48	50	52	54	56	58
British	34	36	38	40	42	44	46	48

Men's Shirts

American	$14^1/_2$	15	$15^1/_2$	16	$16^1/_2$	17	$17^1/_2$	18
Continental	37	38	39	41	42	43	44	45
British	$14^1/_2$	15	$15^1/_2$	16	$16^1/_2$	17	$17^1/_2$	18

MEN'S SHOES

American	7	8	9	10	11	12	13
Continental	39½	41	42	43	44½	46	47
British	6	7	8	9	10	11	12

INDEX

A

A&J's Farm Stand, 127
ACC (American Craft Council)
   Craft Fair, 83, 92
Accommodations, 13–16
Adolfo, 32–33
Adrienne Vittadini, 55
Agnes B., 154
Airports, 17, 111–12, 141,
   185–86
Air travel, 17
Alessi, 107
Alpine sheets and towels, 104
American Craft Council, 83, 84
American Hand, 126
American Tourister, 33–34
Amtrak, 17–18, 186, 188
Ancestors, tracing your, 24
Anne Klein II, 48, 240
Ann Taylor, 155
Anokhi, 154
Antique Center, 102
Antique Center of Northampton,
   70
Antiques, 61–81, 102, 119–23,
   130, 132, 152, 156, 159–60,
   176, 179, 183, 189, 195,
   198, 207, 212, 218, 219,
   226, 231, 234, 235, 247
   auctions, 61–65, 160, 208
   centers, 4, 5, 70–81
   consignment shops, 66–67
   information sources, 67–68
   shows and fairs, 1–2, 69–70
   tag sales, 65–66, 111, 218
Antiques Gallery, 179
Apple cider, 233–34
Appleseed's, 176
April Cornell, 4, 115, 157, 171,
   211
Arlington (VT), 230–31
Arlington Gallery, 231
Armani Exchange, 151
Aromatherapy, 160
Artful Hand, 90
Art galleries, on Cape Cod (MA),
   189, 192, 218
Ashley Falls (CT), 79
Attic Treasures, 119
Augusta, 221

Aunt Leah's, 208
Avenue Victor Hugo Bookshop,
   162

B

Balcony, The , 221
Bally, 34
Banana Republic, 34–35
Bannister Shoe, 35
Barbizon, 35
Barnidge & McEnroe, 124
Barn, The, 105–6
Baskets, 85–86, 94
   lightship, 206–7, 209–10
Bass, 35
Battenkill Plaza, 229
BCBG, 36
Beach needs, 189, 193, 200,
   209
Beacon Hill, 72, 155–56
Beauty supplies, 42, 160–61
Bed, Bath & Beyond, 153
Beer, 161
Ben & Jerry Factory, 233
Benetton, 37
Bennington (VT), 227–28
Bennington Museum, 227
Bennington Potters' Yard,
   227–28
Bergman, Robin L., 84
Berkshire Crafts Fair, 84
Birdhouses, 87–88, 94–95
Black & Decker, 37, 245
Black Swan Antiques, 75–76
Bloomingdale's, 166
Blueberries + Granite, 246
Boat travel and cruises, 7–8,
   19–20. *See also* Ferries
Bon Ton, 207
Bookstore, 39
Bookstores, 39, 115–16, 124,
   154, 161–65, 180, 210
Boston, 137–74
   accommodations, 142–44
   antiques, 72, 159–60
   bookstores, 154, 161–65
   department stores, 166–70
   home furnishings, 171–72
   information sources, 145
   malls, 172–73

254

ABOUT THE AUTHOR

Suzy Gershman is an author and a journalist who has worked in the fiber and fashion industry since 1969 in both New York and Los Angeles, and has held editorial positions at *California Apparel News, Mademoiselle, Gentleman's Quarterly,* and *People* Magazine, where she was West Coast Style editor. She writes regularly for various magazines and her new essays on retailing are text for Harvard Business School. She frequently appears on network and local television; she is a contributing editor to *Travel Weekly.*

Mrs. Gershman lives in Connecticut with her husband, author Michael Gershman, and their son, Aaron. Michael Gershman also contributes to the *Born to Shop* pages.

Want to Go Shopping with Suzy Gershman?

What does Suzy Gershman do on vacation? She goes shopping, of course. But she takes people with her. If you've ever dreamed about shopping with the world's most famous shopper, this could be your chance.

Several times a year, **Born to Shop Tours** venture forth to Suzy's favorite destinations when she takes time to really show off her best finds. The pace is busy but relaxed compared to her regular schedule; several trips are booked through cruise lines to maximize the relaxation possibilities and to cut down on the stresses of transportation and dealing with luggage . . . but you do have to carry your own shopping bags.

Excursions often include lunch at just the right charming spot (perfect for resting tired feet), trips into back rooms and private warehouses not often seen by the public, or opportunities to buy at special discounted rates reserved just for Suzy's guests.

While the schedule varies from year to year (last year, she hosted a shop-a-thon on the QE2, there's almost always a trip to Hong Kong, a trip to New York, and a Mediterranean cruise or two. Space is limited to ensure the intimacy of the group and experience. To find out about current plans or to inquire about arranging your own tour, call Giants at 800/442-6871; ask for Bonnie.

Frommer's Born to Shop guides are available from your favorite bookstore or directly from Macmillan Publishing USA. For credit card orders, call 1-800-428-5331 (AMEX, MC and VISA).

Name _____

Address _____ Phone _____

City _____ State _____

Please send me the following **Frommer's Born to Shop** guides:

Quantity	Title	Price
_____	Born to Shop France	$14.95
_____	Born to Shop Great Britain	$14.95
_____	Born to Shop Hong Kong	$14.95
_____	Born to Shop London	$14.95
_____	Born to Shop Mexico	$14.95
_____	Born to New York	$14.95
_____	Born to Shop Italy	$14.95
_____	Born to Shop New England	$14.95
_____	Born to Shop Paris	$14.95

Available in Fall 1997

_____	Born to Shop Caribbean Ports of Call	$14.95

Total for **Frommer's Born to Shop** Guides $ _____
Please include applicable sales tax

Add $3.00 for first book's S & H, $1.00 per additional book:
$ _____

Total payment: $ _____

Check or Money Order enclosed. Offer valid in the United States only. Please make payable to Macmillan Publishing USA.

Send orders to:
Macmillan Publishing USA
201 West 103rd Street
Attn: Order Department
Indianapolis, IN 46290

BS96